ALL OF CREATION

UNDERSTANDING OUR PLANET AND HOW WE CAN HELP

WRITTEN BY **BETSY PAINTER**

WITH **JOSH MOSEY**

ILLUSTRATED BY **MUTI**

ZONDERkidz

To my nieces, Maisy, Winslow, and Rosie.
May you always wonder at God's good creation.
Here's to leaving it in better shape for you.
—B. P.

———————

To my wife and daughters, who are my favorite parts
of creation and the reason it's important to me that
we keep the planet nice for a long, long time.
—J. M.

CONTENTS

INTRODUCTION

The earth is the Lord's, and everything in it.

—PSALM 24:1 (NIV)

What's your earliest memory in nature? For me, I was wrist-deep in dirt, sitting uphill from a creek lined with oaks and willows. With my mom's garden shovel, I scooped up dirt and molded it into an anthill, then sprinkled grass into the nearby hole to make a bed for grasshoppers. It was an ant and grasshopper duplex.

Even from a young age, I was filled with the wonder of creation. Everything I saw and touched was made by God, from the rocks I picked out to the grasshoppers I caught between my fingers. I took great pleasure in my responsibility to care for the critters in my yard as I built them homes.

God has built us a remarkable home, this planet Earth. We can see creation in a lot of ways: from something to use up like money to nice scenery as we go about our days. In this book, though, I

want to show you a different way to see creation. It's not a *new* view. In fact, it's an ancient way of seeing and interacting with nature that's part of the long history of the Christian faith.

This book is an invitation to connect with nature, wonder at the world, and worship its Maker in a biblical way. I hope that after reading it, you'll have even more love in your heart for God's creation. I also hope you'll learn to see nature as the complicated jumble of beauty that it is, and that you'll want to treat it with the kindness we were designed to show.

> Taking care of creation is not a new idea. In fact, it's the very first responsibility God gave to the very first people on the planet!

Right after God made Adam, he put him in the garden "to work it and take care of it" (Genesis 2:15 NIV). Before sin entered the picture, God gave people good work to do. We've never stopped being responsible for working and caring for creation. We were made to help it grow and reflect God's glory. More than that, we were made to care for the needs of all people, especially those whose needs are the greatest and who are sometimes least able to help themselves.

But how? How do we reconnect to God's original purpose for us?

To do this well, it helps to understand how the planet's systems work. We'll explore what the best available science reveals to us about a bunch of different environments, from wetlands to mountains. When I built the ant and grasshopper homes, my motivation was right, but I was wrong about their habitat needs. The ants never noticed their carefully crafted hills, and the grasshoppers (ungratefully) bounded away from their beds. Likewise, without the right knowledge, our work can miss the mark. However, when we study and know creation well, we can help it grow and protect it better.

Each chapter in the book covers a specific habitat or system in our planet. You'll learn what each ecosystem or area is like, why it's important, and the problems it faces. We'll also explore biblical themes and lessons that show us the wonder of our Maker's creativity and provision. And finally, you'll get practical tips for how you—yes, YOU!—can make a difference.

The goal of this layout is to help connect our hearts with our actions. There are so many things you can do, it's easy to get overwhelmed, but that feeling is not going to be helpful. Remember the goal: to simplify what we can and improve our focus on what's important. Let's live humbly and be thankful for the blessings God has given us. It's a daily challenge, and it affects everything, from the stuff we buy (or don't buy) to our daily habits (like showering) to the things we notice (like litter). How we treat the planet is deeply related to becoming people who treat others as more important than ourselves (Philippians 2:3–4).

There are some people out there who either don't understand the problems facing our environment or don't care about them. I have been working with both Christian ministry and environmental conservation (a fancy term for trying to save the planet) for long enough to know that the problems are real and that God has entrusted us with a job to do. Like Adam in the garden, we can take joy in the work in front of us. I wrote this book because

I believe my family in the faith (that includes you!) has the reason, the hope, and the resources to make a difference.

We have a chance to put the gospel into action and love things back to life. It's time for Christians everywhere to step onto the scene amid a struggling creation, roll up our sleeves, and get "wrist-deep in dirt" to show the world that we care about our mutual home. Let's look at planet Earth as Christ does: with plans and visions for restoration and healing, with the never-ending hope of a Savior who makes all things new.

We really can make a difference! Are you ready to start?

Join me in this prayer before we begin . . .

Loving Lord of heaven and earth,

Thank You for the detail, care, and love You put into creating planet Earth. Thank You for sharing this living work of art, a beautiful masterpiece, with us and giving us the eyes, ears, and minds to study and delight in all of creation with You. Remind us to appreciate creation's gifts with gratitude and a gentle touch. Help us do our part in our own ways to keep the earth alive and well for right now, and for the future.

Please give us the Holy Spirit to renew our minds so we see

the world as You do. Show us where Your earth is broken, lead us to those who lack necessities like food and water, and help us work together as a community of faith to heal and restore. We celebrate Your awesome works—from the vast oceans and forests to the tiny planktons and bugs— and want to work alongside You and in worship of You. Fill the earth with the knowledge of Your glory and the hope of the promised new heaven and new earth through Your Son, Jesus.

In His wonderful name we pray,

Amen.

CHAPTER ONE

FRESH WATER

Our Most Precious and Scarce Resource

He makes springs pour water into the ravines; it flows between the mountains. . . . He waters the mountains from his upper chambers; the land is satisfied by the fruit of his work.

PSALM 104:10, 13

Picture a waterfall running over towers of rock. Mist rises in the sunlight, casting rainbows around the falls. Or imagine waking up during a thunderstorm, as the rain sprays against your window like God is aiming His garden hose at your house. Water is breathtaking and awe-inspiring, but there's not enough of it for everyone who needs it.

It's easy to take water for granted. Anytime you want it, you can get it from the kitchen sink. We wash our hands with it, take showers in it, and even keep it in the toilet. It rains from the sky, runs along in rivers, and fills lakes, ponds, and puddles. It seems like it's always available, but not having access to clean water is one of the

most urgent environmental issues in the world today.

Wait a minute, you might think. *Look at any globe and you can see that most of the world's surface is covered by water!*

Good point! About 70 percent of the earth's surface is covered by water. Then why is water shortage a problem? Most of the water on the planet is salt water, meaning it's undrinkable. The oceans and seas all contain salt water, leaving only 3 percent of the earth's water fresh. Unfortunately, most of this water is frozen at the North and South Poles, which means only a piddly 1 percent is reasonably within reach.

WHAT IS FRESH WATER?

Fresh water is water that has less than 1,000 milligrams per liter of dissolved salts—which is a scientific way of saying it is basically saltless. This includes streams, rivers, ponds, and lakes, as well as glaciers, ice sheets, and icebergs. Another vital source of fresh water is found underground, in layers of porous rock—which is full of holes but holds water like a sponge—called **aquifers**. When it rains, water seeps down through the soil into the aquifer, refilling or recharging it. This groundwater is drawn up by wells and is especially important for our drinking supply and for irrigating (watering) crops.

Clean Water Challenges

Even with the limits on our fresh water supply (it's only 1 percent of the water in the world!), the real challenge is getting fresh water to everyone who needs it. More than two billion people lack access to safe drinking water.[1] That's about double the population of North and South America combined—about one quarter of the earth's total population—without drinkable water! Without water, people can't cook or bathe. Plus, we need to drink water to survive. Can you imagine spending hours of your day walking to get water for your family? That is the reality for many women and children who could be spending that valuable time working or in school.

How bad is the clean water situation? Let's look at a few examples—one overseas and a couple closer to home—to put things in perspective.

US Water Contamination: the Cuyahoga River and Flint, Michigan

Not long ago, the United States had a serious problem with pollution levels in its lakes and rivers. In the 1960s, the Cuyahoga River in Ohio was so filthy with oil leaks and runoff from factories that it burst into flames. This event became a symbol of the American environmental movement and helped start the first Earth Day. After the passing of the **Clean Water Act** in 1972, and extensive work cleaning up and plugging sources of pollution, the river began to recover.

More recently, in 2014, residents in Flint, Michigan, reported that the water in their homes looked dirty, smelled foul, and tasted

Aquifers and Wells

LAKE

ARTISAN WELL

FLOWING ARTISAN WELL

WATER TABLE WELL

CONFINING LAYER

UNCONFINED AQUIFER

CLAY

BEDROCK

CONFINED AQUIFER

bad—an obvious sign that something was wrong with the water. But even after citizens brought the water problem to the attention of officials, nothing was done about it until the case made it to the federal court in 2016. At the time, 44.5 percent of the residents lived below the poverty line, and many of those affected were from minority groups.[2]

Environmental problems like bad drinking water have historically affected people of color in the United States more heavily than those belonging to the white majority of the country. This is partly because of unfair laws that were drawn up so the Black community and other people of color couldn't buy property in the more expensive parts of town. Although these laws have now mostly been repealed (cancelled), the people who live in the poorer parts of town haven't been able to move out because they can't afford to live elsewhere. It's all part of something called "environmental racism," and it isn't fair or right.

By the time the government finally started taking action, thousands of children had been given lead-contaminated water for over a year,[3] which is especially upsetting since lead is really bad for growth and development.

Exposure to lead can cause lower IQ and an inability to pay attention. It can also cause hearing and speech problems. None of these things are going to help kids do better in school or help

An aquifer is an underground layer of rock that acts like a sponge. Humans rely on aquifers for drinking water. These stony sponges allow water to move up through the saturated rock and sediment, providing about 37 percent of our drinking water!

them find good jobs later in life, so they probably won't be able to afford to live somewhere nicer than the places that exposed them to lead in the first place. It's a problem that risks repeating itself again and again.

A Look at India's Water Challenge

India's freshwater situation is a challenging puzzle to solve. The country's water supply is tied to its wild, up-and-down weather, which releases not enough and then too much water depending on the season. Heat shocks and absent rains cause dry spells, while annual **monsoons** bring extreme rainfall and damaging floods. If the monsoons arrive late and last for a shorter period, city **reservoirs** run the risk of drying up. In some cases, the water supply reaches zero. This happened in 2019 in Chennai, India, when the four main reservoirs to the city ran dry, causing a severe water crisis. At the time, twenty-one other Indian cities were also threatened with a dwindling water supply.[4]

In northern India, the Ganges River runs from the Himalayas to the Bay of Bengal. It holds enough water to meet the needs of

four hundred million people[5] (more than the population of the United States!), but it's notoriously polluted. Trash, toxic waste, and raw sewage surge into the river from numerous sources, contaminating its supply and causing deadly diseases.

What makes India's water challenges even greater is the dense population. People living upstream want to make sure they have the water they need, but that means the people living downstream won't have enough. It would be nice to live in a world where everyone shared things equally with those in need (we should all try to make *this* that world), but people get especially desperate when they don't have basic things like water.

Whether the challenges come from crazy climates or from not having access to the same resources, our brothers and sisters living in disadvantaged countries are often hit the hardest.

Have you ever been tempted to take more of something for yourself—pizza, birthday cake, bacon, whatever— even if it means that not everyone will have as much?

Our Responsibility

What happens if we fail to clean up our water sources? Rivers burst into flames. People get sick and pass away. If we aren't wise with how we use and save water, especially in regions where water dries up for part of the year, our water sources can shrink to scary-low levels.

Water justice in the US means doing something about the water issues and protecting clean water sources with the same care and sense of importance for every community. It shouldn't matter who lives there or how much money those people make. We need to make sure that people who live at the edges

We have laws that are designed to protect our water sources. What do you think would be a fair punishment for people who break those laws?

of society are taken care of, but we can't stop with people who live in the US. There are literally billions of people all around the world who need clean water but can't get it.

A Biblical Perspective

When we see a community in need of fresh water, we have an opportunity to show that community what God is like. In the book of Matthew, Jesus said that when we offer a cup of water to someone in need, it's as if we were giving the Messiah Himself a drink (25:37–40). Jesus is very serious about taking care of people's physical needs, and we should be too. God invites you and me to participate in providing fresh water for His people, and when we do, we can be confident that we are becoming more like Christ.

Water Connects Us

As we learn in Genesis 1:2, while creation was still empty and formless, God's Spirit was "hovering over the face of the waters."

God had a plan for water to take care of all life on earth. Amazingly, every water molecule God created in the beginning is still a part of the water cycle today! Around the planet, water evaporates, condenses into clouds, then falls back to the earth as rain or snow. This natural circulation of water connects the seas and rivers with the forests, grasslands, wetlands, and deserts.

It also connects them to you and me. Water is the foundational force—the initial ingredient through which the rest of creation was built—that binds each ecosystem to another. Without it, life would fail. When we pollute our water or use too much of it, we mess with the systems God set in place to give and support life.

Water Sustains Us

Humans aren't just dependent on the water *around* us. We're connected to the earth by the water *inside* us too! Our bodies contain around 60 percent water, and our brain cells are about 85 percent water. We literally can't think without it. We can't survive more than several days without drinking it. It's how we naturally cool our bodies through sweat and how we express emotion through tears. God *designed* us to need water. It's pretty incredible to think God created our bodies with water, to continually need water, and to get water from His creation.

Do you ever think about your dependence on water and the natural world?

Scripture shows us that it matters to God that people have clean water to drink. In the book of Exodus, God caused water to gush forth from a rock in the wilderness. God made it possible for Jacob to buy some land and build a well to supply water to his community—a well that was famous hundreds of years later when Jesus walked the earth. God gives us so much more than just the water we drink. He takes care of us spiritually too!

Water Renews Us Spiritually

Throughout the Bible, God uses water metaphorically—as a symbol of something greater—to show us our need for spiritual renewal, which means returning to God to keep our faith strong. Just as God designed our physical bodies to rely on water, our spirits cannot fully live without God's presence inside us.

Let's look at the practice of baptism. Whether your church baptizes someone by sprinkling or dunking, through faith the water is a sacred sign of God's cleansing us of our sins, the rebirth of our souls, and our welcome into God's family. Jesus also used water to wash the disciples' feet, and when he did Peter learned he had to let Jesus wash his spirit (which meant humbling himself and becoming "clean" from the inside out so he could do what Jesus taught) to share in the life of holiness with God the Father. In all these examples God chose water, with its cleansing abilities, to physically show our need for spiritual change.

God offers us peace in the presence of water. Psalm 23:2–3 says, "He leads me beside still waters. He restores my soul." When we take time to sit by a stream and pray, the peace of God settles over us like calm waters. When we play in ocean waves or swim in a pond, we wake up to God's joy in creation. Someday we'll enjoy life in a perfect new place, but until then, as Christians, we have a responsibility to respect and protect Earth and its water.

How can you show God that you're thankful for the water He's provided?

When we consider what a gift water is—a life-giving, satisfying, make-us-clean-again gift—we see how important it is for us to take good care of our water sources and supplies. We can't take water for granted or assume that everyone has it just because we do. God gives us good gifts like water because He knows we need it, but also so we can share those gifts with others so they'll know Him too! It's our job as God's followers to make sure everyone has clean, accessible water.

HOW YOU CAN MAKE A DIFFERENCE

CONSERVE WATER AND CREATE LIFESTYLE HABITS

You can make a difference with how you use water every day! Think about the water you use and thank God for ways He's blessed you. Here are a few ways you can be extra thoughtful when it comes to using water.

Avoid faucet fouls

◊ Turn off your faucet while it's not in use. Running water while brushing your teeth? That's a faucet foul! Mindfully turn it off.

Sniff and re-wear your clothes

◊ Very few parents or caregivers love doing laundry, but we all wear clothes, so the laundry must get done. But does an item of clothing need to go into the hamper after one use? Probably not. You can save water by hanging up your clothes after use to air them out. Toss them into the wash only when your eyes (or nose) confirm they're dirty.

Bathroom challenge

◊ Limit your time in the shower to three to eight minutes, or as brief as possible. Pick a couple of songs and challenge yourself to finish showering before they're over (singing along is encouraged).

Investigate your pipes

💧 Want an excuse to explore your house? Crawl under each sink in your home and see if there are any leaky pipes. Leaky pipes waste water and can lead to weird smells and rotten floorboards. The sooner these are fixed, the better.

💧 Test your toilet for leaks. Remove the toilet tank lid, add ten drops of food coloring into the tank, replace the lid (don't flush), wait fifteen minutes, and then check the toilet bowl. If the water is colored, you have a leak and need to have it fixed.

ENGAGE WITH YOUR LOCAL WATER SOURCES

Water issues are global, but it's helpful to think locally.

Explore local rivers, lakes, and streams

💧 The writer of Genesis mentioned the rivers flowing out of Eden by name—Tigris, Euphrates, Pishon, and Gihon. Do you know the names of the bodies of water in your area?

💧 Have a caregiver contact your local utility company to ask where your water is sourced from. Visit and pray by these vital freshwater ecosystems.

Litter cleanups, plus outdoor sports

- Organize a litter cleanup by foot, kayak, or canoe with your church or neighborhood. Bring trash bags and map out a route. Make an awesome poster or use social media to let other people know what's going on.
- Go plogging! Plogging started in Sweden but has picked up all over the world. The word is a mashup of the Swedish words *plocka upp* (which means "pick up") and *jogga* (which means "jog"). So go for a jog and pick up some trash! Every piece of litter you pick up is something that won't end up in our rivers and lakes.

SUPPORT WATER-FOCUSED NONPROFITS

Consider supporting one of these groups to help your neighbors around the world. You could raise funds by starting a "water only" challenge, where people donate money for each day you drink only water instead of sports drinks, juice, or soda.

- **Living Water International** is a faith-based organization that has completed more than 21,000 clean-water projects globally.
- **World Hope International** brings clean water, energy, and economic empowerment to vulnerable populations.
- **Swechha** is a youth-led organization in India that cleans up rivers and uses the litter to make or "upcycle" merchandise.

DO THE WATER POLLUTION CLEANUP
EXPERIMENT AT HOME

Want a better understanding of the problems involved in cleaning up water pollution? Try this experiment.

Supplies

- 4 clear containers, such as plastic cups or glass jars
- Dirt/soil
- Food coloring
- Candy wrappers, bits of plastic, and other trash
- Coffee grounds, tomato sauce, or other food scraps
- 1 mesh strainer
- 2 coffee filters
- 3 sheets of paper towel
- 1 spoon
- 1 tray (for the things you'll scoop out of the water

Directions

1. Fill two of the containers about half full of clean water.
2. Observe how they look and smell.
3. Add some dirt/soil, food coloring, and food scraps to the water in one of the containers. Stir it around with the spoon.
4. Make more observations. How does that container look and smell now?
5. Begin cleaning up the container, using the spoon to remove whatever you can from the polluted water.

6. Next, use the mesh strainer to clean up your polluted water by pouring the dirty water into one of the empty containers.
7. Make an observation. How effective was the strainer at cleaning the water? How does the water look and smell now?
8. Now pour the polluted water through the coffee filters into the remaining empty container.
9. Make an observation. How effective were the coffee filters at removing the pollution from the water?
10. Compare the container that had none of the dirty bits added to the one you've spent time cleaning up. Can you tell them apart?

Reflection Questions

- Compare the water levels between the final two containers. Which one has more?
- Would you want to drink the water that's been cleaned up? Why or why not?
- Which bits of pollution were the easiest to remove? Which ones were the hardest?
- What do you think might happen if you added other pollutants like vegetable oil or juice to the water before attempting to clean it up? Feel free to try the experiment again to see what happens. Just make sure you use the paper towels to clean up any mess you made!

CHAPTER TWO

ENDANGERED SPECIES

The Plants and Animals on Our Watch

Praise the LORD, all his works everywhere in his dominion.

PSALM 103:22 (NIV)

Did you know we've identified around 1.2 million different living creatures on the planet? But incredibly, it's estimated that there may be as many as 8.7 million or more in existence.[1] Basically, for every living creature we know about, there may be five or six more we *don't* know about!

Unfortunately, many of these species go extinct every day, often without us even knowing about it. The causes can be natural, but the current extinction rate for species—the speed at which different animals are disappearing from our planet—is now tens to hundreds of times higher than the usual rate.[2] Scientists refer to this event as the Sixth Mass Extinction and say it's caused by humans and it's speeding up.[3]

WHAT ARE ENDANGERED SPECIES?

Endangered species are plants and animals whose group numbers are shrinking as they move closer and closer to extinction. The risk of extinction is ranked by different levels: least concern, near threatened, vulnerable, endangered, critically endangered, extinct in the wild, and extinct. A plant or animal can become extinct in one region or they can disappear entirely from the globe. In the US, many are protected by the **Endangered Species Act**.

Can you imagine a world where no tigers roam or blue whales swim? We share the earth with many creatures that are now on the brink of existing only in memory. We're used to having them around, but we need to be intentional to make sure there's space for them to stay.

The last big extinction event that scientists talk about happened with the dinosaurs, but what if we're in the middle of another extinction event?

Biodiversity at Play

Once an endangered species is gone, it leaves an empty hole in its habitat—the home it shares with other living things. It can no longer do the special job it once did to keep the **ecosystem** balanced.

Sometimes another creature in the habitat can step in and perform the needed position, like a backup player waiting on the bench to enter a sports match. But as we lose more species, the pool of available replacements dries up. This is why having a lot of different species around—also known as **biodiversity**—is so, so, sooooo important to the planet. The natural world thrives when it's bountifully biodiverse. As we lose each species, the biodiversity of its habitat lessens, and the stability breaks down. The benefits that ecosystem provides—like clean air, water, food, medicines, and recreation—are then at risk.

An ecosystem is an interconnected community made up of living things (animals and organisms) and their non-living environment, working together as a unit. Different areas of the planet have completely different kinds of ecosystems.

Keystone Species

Let's talk about sea otters. With their round little faces and the fact that they hold hands while they sleep, it's easy to see why so many people love sea otters. But did you know that they also have the warmest fur of any mammal? In fact, sea otters have two layers of fur; the inner layer is dark and dense—with about 100,000 hairs per square inch—and the outer layer is lighter and traps air, so the sea otter's skin never even gets wet![4]

When sea otters were hunted almost to extinction during a boom in the fur trade in the eighteenth and nineteenth centuries, the sea urchins they ate were no longer kept in check. Spiky clusters of urchins took over underwater forests of kelp, destroying the homes of many other animals like turtles and octopuses. That's because otters are a *keystone species*, a species that has a bigger-than-you-might-expect impact on the health of a habitat.[5]

Beavers are another keystone species. Through the lodges and dams they build, beavers can change the flow of streams and rivers, creating huge wetland areas that are used by all kinds of other animals.

Endangered species projects often focus on the charismatic species, like leopards, elephants, and pandas. This can be a good conservation tactic because most of these **megafauna**, as they're called, are keystone species—and by protecting them, many other species are saved. But an endangered species can be anything from a bird, mammal, or tree to a fungi, snail, sponge, or insect.

Consider the *Pisaster ochraceus*, or purple sea star, which is another keystone species. As animals go, purple sea stars aren't nearly as cute as sea otters (who sometimes eat them). In fact, they are downright strange. When a purple sea star wants to eat something too large to swallow whole, they turn their stomachs inside out over their prey and digest it before swallowing it. Weird and gross, but kind of amazing too, right? And without them, the biodiversity within their habitat goes down, because the mussels the sea stars eat start

growing in number and eating the creatures around them, until not much more than the mussels remain.

No matter its size or appearance, each species plays a purposeful and significant role in the function of its natural home. Every species matters in our interconnected ecosystems, and each requires our attention when it's threatened with extinction, especially when this endangerment happens due to human actions.

Causes of Endangerment

The greatest threats to endangered species and the associated loss of biodiversity are connected to human activity. These threats include habitat loss, overexploitation, pollution, invasive species, and climate change.

Habitat Loss

Habitat loss is the leading cause of extinction. When we destroy, shrink, or use up the land where wildlife lives in order to build houses and shopping centers, wild animals become crowded in the broken-up land and are forced to live closer to humans (and the humans aren't the ones who suffer). When wildlife and humans are nearer to each other, what's known as *human-wildlife conflict* increases.

For example, check out what's happening between farmers and snow leopards.

Snow leopards are big cats with gray-green eyes and full, white fur covered in black rosettes. These gorgeous big cats are disappearing in the cliffs and rocks of the Himalayas. Based on the available research data, scientists think there's only 4,500 to 7,500 left on the entire planet.[6] One reason is that their prey—blue sheep, ibex, marmots, pikas, and hares—are also diminishing. As a result, the snow leopards will often attack farmers' livestock for food instead, and the farmers fight back by killing the snow leopards to protect their livelihoods. As humans continue to move into wildlife territory, we need to establish new and creative ways of living alongside the animals, like using livestock fencing that's designed to keep big cats out.

How would you feel if a group of animals moved into your house without your permission? Where would you go?

Another victim of human expansion is the Ili pika. These rare little mammals were discovered in the Tianshan Mountains of

northwestern China in 1983. At about eight inches long, with large ears and a round face, the Ili pika looks like a cross between a bunny and a stuffed teddy bear. They live high in the mountains and eat grasses, herbs, and other mountain plants, but their habitat is at risk due to human interaction. Farmers moving into the Ili pikas' home means new predators in the form of farm dogs. Between that and **air pollution** caused by humans, these fuzzy animals are listed by the International Union for Conservation of Nature as endangered and vulnerable to extinction.[7] And unfortunately, no one has initiated any action plans to save Ili pikas from disappearing from the earth.

Overexploitation

Overexploitation is a major contributor to species endangerment. What is overexploitation? It's when people hunt and harvest wildlife faster than the population of that wildlife can reproduce. This includes when people illegally trade and kill animals for their fur or other products. Poachers—people who hunt animals illegally— kill tens of thousands of elephants in Africa and Asia every year for their ivory tusks. After the US, China, and other countries banned the ivory trade, demand for tusks steadily decreased, but illegal poaching and ivory trading still exist, mostly because some people don't enforce the laws since poachers and traders pay them not to.[8]

Elephants aren't the only victims. Poachers kill rhinos for their horns, which are used in traditional Chinese medicines and are believed to have healing powers. But guess what? Rhino horns are mostly made of keratin, the same protein that's in fingernails. Scientists have found little to no evidence that rhino horns have medicinal benefits.[9]

Diseases

Are you ready to learn a new word? **Zoonotic**. It refers to the kind of diseases that can jump from animals living in the wild to animals on farms to people. Zoonotic diseases like Ebola,

West Nile virus, and Lyme disease are happening more and more. When the world was shut down due to the COVID-19 pandemic, many people believed that the disease either came from a laboratory or from animal hosts like bats or pangolins.[10]

Pangolins are gentle mammals with scales that protect them like armor. Their scales are prized for use in traditional medicines, and their meat is considered fine dining in some cultures. For this reason, they're the most illegally trafficked—traded, smuggled, and sold—mammal in the world and are threatened with extinction. Within the illegal trade known as the black market, pangolins are crammed together in unclean cages, creating a prime opportunity for disease to spread. This is one reason why the COVID-19 virus was initially suspected to have jumped from animals to people through pangolins.[11]

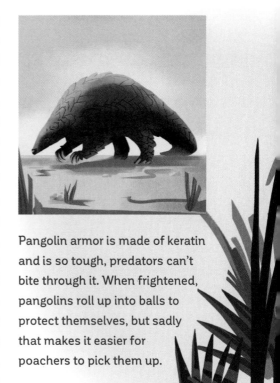

Pangolin armor is made of keratin and is so tough, predators can't bite through it. When frightened, pangolins roll up into balls to protect themselves, but sadly that makes it easier for poachers to pick them up.

Widespread pandemics and more local forms of disease are tragic examples of what can happen when we don't manage wild-life responsibly. When we care for wildlife well, we also help prevent future pandemics and keep people from getting zoonotic diseases. We must do better to take care of all creatures for their survival—and ours.

A Biblical Perspective

In Genesis 2:19 we read, "Now out of the ground the LORD God had formed every beast of the field and every bird of the heavens and brought them to the man to see what he would call them." Our very first task as humans was to see, get to know, and then name each of our fellow creatures. God could have named them, but He wanted our compassionate creativity involved in this joyful act. And we are still discovering and naming species today!

God's Creativity on Display

Biodiversity and the many different kinds of life on earth show off the endless creativity of the Maker, who made every living thing through and for Jesus (Colossians 1:16). How cool is that! Every plant, worm, chipmunk, and flower—whatever you might see during your daily walk—was made through Jesus. Each one has a godly charm that points right back to Christ.

What is your favorite part of creation? How can you thank Jesus for being the reason and the method that object or creature was made?

There's actually a fancy word for this that gets tossed around in Bible schools. It's called *haecceity* (pronounced *heck-say-ity*), and it means the "thisness" of any one thing. It's what makes your favorite book or T-shirt different from all the other books and T-shirts that look like it in the world. The truth is that every created thing—every animal and plant and person and bit of creation—is unique and original, made to be the way it is by God Himself.

And the way God created every little thing says something to us about God, just like a work of art tells us something about the artist. Romans 1:20 says, "For his invisible attributes, namely, his eternal power and divine nature, have been clearly perceived, ever since the creation of the world, in the things that have been made." Each species is a part of the puzzle of God's glory in nature and should be kept safe and loved, simply because they were made by God.

Our Humble Dominion

Beyond naming plants and animals, God also gave us dominion over every living thing. "Be fruitful and multiply and fill the earth and subdue it, and have dominion over the fish of the sea and over the birds of the heavens and over every living thing that moves on the earth" (Genesis 1:28).

What's dominion? It comes from an ancient word for house and refers to someone being responsible for taking care of that house. Think about your room for a minute. It's nicer to spend time in your room when it's clean, right? You don't own your room, but you are responsible for making sure there aren't half-eaten burritos hidden under the dresser or piles of unwashed clothes on the bed or sticky patches of dried soda on the floor. No one wants to live like that, right? But it takes time and effort to clean up after yourself if you want to live in a clean room.

Now let's think bigger. You don't just have dominion over your room. God has given you (and every other human) shared dominion over the earth. To do that well requires us to lead other people by example. You know who was great at leading by example? Jesus!

Jesus cleansed, healed, and restored everywhere He went. Even though He was God, He humbled himself (Philippians 2:8) and did the dirty jobs no one else wanted to do. He came to serve, not to be served (Matthew 20:28), and we are called to be like Him. We are invited to lead humbly as people who care for God's creation. When we do, we can work to make sure that habitats stay biodiverse and stable for future generations and that endangered species are protected. Let's make sure animals don't go extinct if we can prevent them from doing so!

Psalm 145:9 says the Lord's "tender mercies are over all His works" (NKJV). God cares for every living creature He has made. He made every single one—including you!—unique. (Haecceity!) We honor God's creation by doing our part to take care of it.

> We get to be God's example to the world, and it's our responsibility to lead like Jesus would.

God has entrusted His creatures into our hands. Think about that for a minute. It's a big responsibility. God is calling us (you!) to safeguard the ways He's made creatures and creation to flourish.

HOW YOU CAN MAKE A DIFFERENCE

ENGAGE WITH LOCAL ENDANGERED SPECIES CONSERVATION

Local species are an irreplaceable part of the biodiversity that makes habitats resilient. Even the less well-known or attractive creatures—worms, snails, mussels, rodents, and cockroaches—do really important jobs in their habitats.

Combat invasive species

Plants and animals that are plopped into an ecosystem from somewhere else, often by humans, and then harm the plants and animals that were there first are called **invasive species**. They can really mess with their new habitats, sometimes even wiping out the species that lived there originally—especially the endangered ones.

- Do you ever go hiking or fishing with your family or friends? That's great! Spending time in nature is a wonderful thing. But make sure you clean your hiking and fishing gear as well as your boat, kayak, or paddleboard before moving to a new location. Nobody wants to be the person who accidently carries an invasive species to where it can cause harm!

- Don't release your pets—like aquarium fish, plants, or other exotic animals—into the wild. Your sweet pet goldfish could grow gigantic and disrupt a lake ecosystem.[12] No joke, this happens!
- Find out which invasive species are causing issues your area. There may be local programs dedicated to fighting these environmental threats that are in need of your help.

GET INVOLVED IN GLOBAL ENDANGERED SPECIES CONSERVATION

Endangered species are all around the world. We can support conservation projects in faraway places by being creative in our own homes.

Learn more about organizations on the frontlines of conservation

Finding creative solutions to human-wildlife conflict is necessary to help people and wildlife coexist as they continually move into closer proximity.

- Follow and donate to the Snow Leopard Trust, which is building predator-proof corrals with herders and creating reserves for wild snow leopard prey in India so the snow leopards don't need to eat the farmers' livestock.
- Save Pangolins supports conservation efforts around the world, granting funds to projects that change the people's behavior behind the illegal pangolin trade. Plus, their website has cool pangolin facts, crafts, and coloring pages!

- **The African Wildlife Foundation** in Uganda prevents the human-wildlife conflict that happens when elephants accidentally trample farmers' crops by creating elephant deterrents, like hanging chili peppers on fences. It's simple and brilliant!
- **The World Wildlife Fund (WWF)** has a "Back a Ranger" project, which helps provide rangers with equipment, training, and resources to prevent wildlife crime.

Think of some ways you can raise money

- Sell your artwork to raise money for one of the organizations above. If you draw, draw the animals you'd like to help save from extinction. Sell your artwork to family and friends. Maybe you could even have an art show at school, or a parent or caregiver could help you set up an online shop.
- Host a bake sale with cookies in the shapes of the animals you want to help. If you can't find a cookie cutter in the shape you need, look up one of the online guides to see how your caregivers can help you make your own. Fun and delicious!
- If drawing or baking aren't your thing, see if your local pizza place will help you out by agreeing to donate a percentage of their sales for a day while you tell all your friends (and your caregivers tell all their social media connections) to get pizza from there!
- If Christmas is around the corner, you could set up a gift wrapping station and have folks donate to your cause in exchange for wrapping their gifts. Bonus points if you wrap gifts in your own wrapping paper featuring your favorite animal!

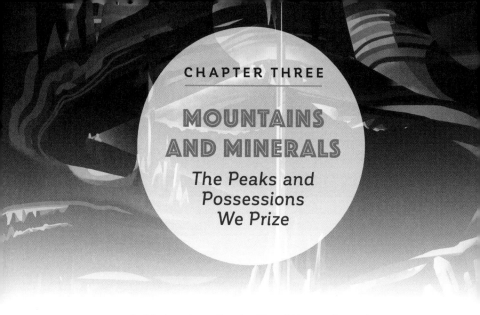

CHAPTER THREE

MOUNTAINS AND MINERALS

The Peaks and Possessions We Prize

In his hand are the depths of the earth, and the mountain peaks belong to him.

PSALM 95:4 (NIV)

Have you ever seen mountains from a distance? The land around you is flat, then you notice something appear on the horizon. As you get closer, what you thought might be a cloud or a hill starts to come into focus. With every step, the mountains get bigger and bigger. And if you venture up them, you might find yourself looking down at clouds of fog beneath you.

Or maybe you've visited a cave or a cavern and seen stalactites (the ones that hang down) and stalagmites (the ones that stick up) and been amazed at God's hidden creativity. Think about all the beautiful things God has buried in the ground, just waiting for us to discover. Diamonds and gemstones are some of the most expensive things in the world, but they're natural wonders made by God.

Where are these amazing things found? In mountains and mines! Before we get into how we use the stuff God's hidden for us to discover, let's talk about mountains and how God made them.

Where Do Mountains Come From?

There are a few different ways mountains show up in the world, but they are all related to tectonic plates in one way or another. **Tectonic plates** are different sections of the earth's crust and upper mantle that float on top of the liquid magma (melted rock) near the earth's core. Let's break that down a bit more.

Think of the earth as a boiled egg. The earth's crust is like the thin shell of the egg. The mantle, which is made of semi-solid rock and magma, is like the white part of the egg. And the yellow bit represents the earth's core, which is made of iron and nickel. Tectonic plates are places where the eggshell has cracked and can float around the surface of the "egg."

When two different plates smash into each other like a car crash in slow motion, they buckle up into mountain ranges. The Appalachian Mountains formed in this way. The tectonic plate that's forced under gets melted and becomes part of the earth's mantle again.

A more jaw-dropping way mountains are formed is through volcanic activity. As tectonic plates move away from each other, magma rises from the cracks and cools as crystals to form igneous rocks. Over time, these rocks grow into volcanic mountains. The Hawaiian

Islands are a great example of active volcanoes turning into ever-growing mountains.

Similar to the water cycle, rocks can cycle through different stages. Over time, weather and vegetation break down the igneous rocks that make up most mountains, turning them into the sedimentary layers of the earth—the parts above the earth's mantle. When enough of those layers stack on top of each other, they get pressed together to form sedimentary rocks. The rocks closest to the earth's hot core get changed by the heat into metamorphic rock. Then when these new rocks melt completely, they become magma. The magma rises through volcanoes and cracks in the earth's crust, and *bam!* We're back where we started!

There are incredible forces at work in the clashing crust and flowing lava of mountain making. Just as amazing are the more subtle, hidden mechanisms behind the formation of

WHAT ARE MINERALS?

Minerals are basically clumps of specific elements (like from the periodic table of the elements) that have bonded together in different, sometimes beautiful, ways. They occur naturally in the earth and are the building blocks of rocks. More than four thousand different minerals have been found on the planet. Some mineral crystals are cut and polished into gems—rubies, emeralds, turquoise, jade, and other precious jewels—but other important minerals form ore deposits containing metals like copper, iron, gold, and silver.

gemstones—rubies, sapphires, opals, malachite, diamonds, and peridots, to name a few—and minerals underground. These natural gifts are dug from the earth and are found strewn throughout our products and possessions. In addition to fancy gemstones used in jewelry, rocks and minerals are found in a ton of things we use every day. Minerals make up the steel and aluminum used in making cars, trains, planes, and boats. You use them whenever you turn on a light (electrical wires!), draw a picture (pencils!), and eat your breakfast (plates and silverware!). We use mineral salt to flavor our food, sodium bicarbonate for baking bread and cakes, and calcium carbonate to calm our stomachs when we've eaten too many cakes.

Where do all these rocks and minerals come from? From the ground beneath your feet! To get to these buried treasures, we rely on mining operations.

The Upside and Downside of Mining

Miners extract gems and minerals from the crust—the outer (eggshell) layer of the earth—so other people can make beautiful jewelry and all kinds of great things. In some communities, mines are the only place to work, and miners make it possible for other parts of the country to have the materials they need to make the things we use. Although it is important to make sure communities have places to work and people have materials to build stuff out of, there are serious downsides to mining too, specifically in how the mining is done.

Blasting techniques, where miners use explosives to uncover the rocks and minerals they need, are especially bad for the land

The Formation of Minerals and Gemstones

Weather eroding the mountain

Slow uplift to the surface

IGNEOUS ROCK

OPAL MALACHITE

Sedimentary layer

Crystallization of magma

RUBY SAPPHIRE

Compaction & cementation

MAGMA CHAMBER

SEDIMENTARY ROCK

DIAMOND   PERIDOTS

Melting

Burial, high temperatures & pressures

Magma from crust and mantle (under all layers)

METAMORPHIC ROCK

where the miners and communities live. Mining sites are required to follow strict rules to keep mine workers safe from toxic gases and other hazards, as well as to prevent significant damage to the environment. But when these rules are ignored, mines can cave in and cause landslides, explosions, and fires, all

of which put people's health in danger. Then once the mine no longer has the rocks and minerals people need, the pits that were blasted and mines that were drilled need to be filled in and the land restored, but these steps don't always happen.

Mountaintop removal is another kind of mining that has some serious problems. It's a relatively new way to get coal out of the earth—and, unfortunately, burning coal causes its own environmental problems. But mountaintop removal is pretty much what it sounds like: blowing up mountain tops. It doesn't only destroy the beauty of the mountains; millions of tons of rock,

If there was a highway to the earth's core (and you were traveling at normal highway speeds), it would take less than twenty minutes to get through the earth's crust. To reach the bottom of a tectonic plate, you'd have to travel for about an hour. But to get to the very center of the earth, it would take around sixty-six hours (two full days plus eighteen more hours) of driving, not counting bathroom breaks.[1]

sand, and coal debris (tiny bits) from the explosions are dumped in the valleys and end up polluting waterways and the atmosphere. This mining practice has caused a lot of arguments in the central Appalachian Mountains, where communities near the mines suffer from an increase in heart diseases, lung cancer, and birth defects.[2]

Because we depend on rocks and minerals for so many daily activities, we likely won't be able to stop mining completely. But like most things that affect the environment, there are ways to go about it that are less harmful in the long run. Lower-impact mining techniques, reuse of mining waste, and filling in and restoring mining sites are a few practices we can support.[3]

Mining Rare Earth Metals

In China, mining rare earth metals—metals with hard-to-pronounce names like lanthanum, cerium, neodymium, and dysprosium that are used to make high-tech gadgets—spiked in the 1990s. If you have a smartphone, a laptop, or a video gaming console, you're using rare earth metals. These metals are also used for things like wind turbines and electric vehicles (EVs). The chemicals used to get these elements out of the earth led to soil and water contamination, and the upturning of the earth scarred the land. After public protests, the Chinese government responded with stricter mining regulations.[4] Many mines were shut down, and local and federal officials led cleanup initiatives that included wastewater treatment facilities and planting vegetation like bamboo and grasses to cover barren areas and stop erosion.[5]

There are often trade-offs when choosing between environmentally conscious products and human needs. EVs and wind turbines are super important to a more promising future for us and the environment, but we must work to ensure that the processes behind making them (like mining rare earth metals, in this case) avoid as much planetary harm as possible. Even eco-friendly goods need accountability from the point where we take the materials out of the earth to the time we hold the finished product in our hands. For example, for the rare earth metals in our electronics, like smartphones and videogaming systems, a solution is to recycle them properly so their parts can be reused for future products.

Our Responsibility

Think again about all the things you use that have minerals and metals in them. How many toys and electronic gadgets do you have? Have you ever considered how those things were made? It isn't wrong to have these things, but we should ask ourselves: What is the cost to the earth?

We can't afford to ignore where our things are coming from, and we can't ignore the communities that suffer when it's part of the process of making our stuff. Even if you aren't the one spending money on these things (thank God for parents and caregivers!), as someone who uses them, you have a role to play in making sure the mines where they come from are working toward safer, less harmful practices. We all need to do our part to keep the land productive for the people who depend on it.

How do you think God feels when people don't fix the things they break? Does it matter if people don't realize the harm they cause?

A Biblical Perspective

Maybe you never thought about metals, minerals, or mining practices before today. But not knowing where something comes from or how it is made doesn't mean you aren't responsible for using it. The fact that our lives benefit from people who destroy the earth (literally blasting it apart in the case of mining operations!) means we need to be thoughtful about how we live. We can change the way we use things and apologize to God for our part in messing up the planet, then we can accept God's grace through the cross, on which Jesus carried our greed and destructive habits.

In Him we can have the wisdom and motivation to make changes. The first step is to start recognizing that the way we treat the environment is a part of holy, godly living. God has given us the ability to take care of the temporary treasures of earth in ways that reflect His goodness, uphold His natural world, and serve the people who rely on it.

God made the minerals and metals as resources for the things we need, but we should be careful not to be greedy or take things just because we want them. And how we get these materials from the earth should match the character of the God who put them there in the first place.

The Mountains and God Protect Us

Many times in Scripture, God's people had to hide in the cliffs and caves of mountains when they were in danger. In Psalm 121, the psalm writer looked up to the hills for a reminder that his help comes from the Lord.

God Himself is compared to the mountains as our refuge and

strong shelter. Psalm 125:2 says, "As the mountains surround Jerusalem, so the LORD surrounds his people both now and forevermore" (NIV). Yet God is greater and sturdier than the most solid mountain range.

In the words of Psalm 46:1–3: "God is our refuge and strength, an ever-present help in trouble. Therefore we will not fear, though the earth give way and the mountains fall into the heart of the sea, though its waters roar and foam and the mountains quake with their surging" (NIV).

Minerals Are God's Unique Creation

Silver, sapphires, opals, and gold—all the precious metals and gems—were made in the earliest days of creation, watched over personally by God. For the one-of-a-kind crystals to grow, each mineral required specific conditions and ingredients: the right mixture of elements, intense pressure, high temperatures, space, and time. John 1:3 says, "Through him all things were made; without him nothing was made that has been made" (NIV). God is the melder of minerals and knows the location of each deposit. How awesome is He to hide beautiful things in the ground for us to discover!

Have you ever found a particularly sparkly rock or stone on the playground or in a park? Maybe you showed it off to your friends or took it home to add to your rock collection. Minerals and gemstones are one of the most dazzling parts of God's creation. Sometimes Christians worry that when we appreciate the beauty in this world, we may be tempted to worship nature instead of its Creator. We can avoid this by remembering that God is way more awesome than anything He's created. Beauty in nature points to its Maker. We can simply say thanks to Him! Then show our gratitude by holding our earthly treasures with open hands— happy not only to show and tell but to share.

Durable Beauty

Precious gems and metals also teach us something about a beauty that outlasts world leaders and kingdoms, hidden away to be discovered only when someone starts digging. It's a lot like how God designed His kingdom to work. Matthew 13:44 says, "The kingdom of heaven is like treasure hidden in a field, which a man found and covered up. Then in his joy he goes and sells all that he has and buys that field." Consider the treasure in this metaphor. Could it be a collection of rubies or other gems buried and discovered in a field?

The treasures of the kingdom of God—salvation, God's promises to always love and forgive us, the home He's preparing for us in the future—are like gemstones in how

What does it say about us when we value things more than their Creator?

long they last and how much they're worth. Gems and precious metals are almost indestructible and last for centuries. Other resources rust or wear out and can be compared to the stuff of this world that eventually breaks. Just think about how quickly electronics break down—and those are made with some of the precious metals we're talking about! But the treasures of God's kingdom will always outshine and outlast (Matthew 6:19–21).

HOW YOU CAN MAKE A DIFFERENCE

PRACTICE ELECTRONIC WASTE (E-WASTE) SOLUTIONS

What if there was an easier way to get things like minerals and rare metals out of the earth? One that didn't involve mining or mountaintop removal? There is. Right now, people have started "mining" from landfills for valuable metals and materials to put back into the production process. Want to join the effort? Just recycle your electronics!

Buy less; practice minimalism

◊ We're constantly tempted by the newest electronics out there (video game systems, televisions, etc.), even when our current ones work fine. You can resist this! Learn to be content with and take care of the stuff you already have.

- Whenever you want to buy something, write down what it is and how much it costs. See if you can borrow or rent the thing you want—some libraries even loan out video games and gaming systems. At the end of the year, add up all the things you wanted but didn't buy. You'll be amazed at how much money you've saved! Plus, you'll feel good about your earth-friendly choices, and that feeling is priceless.

Upcycle

- Upcycling—or creatively reusing things—finds fun, new ways to reuse, share, and swap out our goods. Thrift shops and garage sales are a great place to find new-to-you stuff that still has some life left.

Recycle your electronics properly

- Our electronic gadgets can't just be tossed into our recycling bins. By taking the extra step and finding electronics recycling centers (places like Best Buy and Staples will take e-waste), you can make sure your electronics are given new life. For every million cell phones recycled, we can recover 35 thousand pounds of copper, 772 pounds of silver, 75 pounds of gold, and 33 pounds of palladium.[6]

GO FURTHER IN YOUR MOUNTAIN STUDIES

Understanding how God designed the world to follow certain laws is a great way to appreciate how complex and awesome a creator we have.

Go on a rock hunt

- Rocks are everywhere! They're scattered on the ground around houses and buried just below the surface. Go find a few rocks and see if you can figure out what kind they are: igneous, sedimentary, or metamorphic.
- Ask a teacher or librarian for resources you could use to identify the rocks in your collection. See if they have any educational videos they can suggest to better explain where metals come from or how mountains turn into volcanoes.

Make a Crayon Lava Flow at Home

It's pretty difficult to see the rock cycle in action since parts of it happen deep inside the earth. But you can make your own rock cycle using crayons as sedimentary rock. This experiment will show you what happens when you add heat and pressure, just like rocks experience as they change from one kind to another. This experiment is going to need some parental supervision. Do not try anything without a parent present and paying attention![7]

Supplies

- Old crayons
- Aluminum foil
- A frying pan
- Oven mitts

Directions

1. Peel the paper off your old crayons.
2. Break up the crayons into smaller bits.

3. Line the frying pan with aluminum foil. (No one wants melted crayon all over their nice frying pan.)
4. Place the crayon bits into the frying pan.
5. Make an observation. What shape are the crayon bits before the experiment begins?
6. Have an adult heat the frying pan over medium heat until the crayons begin to melt.
7. Using the oven mitts, carefully tilt the pan to create a lava flow.
8. Remove the pan from the heat. Turn off the stove. Let everything cool completely. Don't touch the melted crayon!
9. Make an observation. How did the crayon change when heat was applied?

Reflection Questions

- How might cooling the crayon quickly in ice water change its appearance compared to allowing it to cool slowly?
- What would happen if you used more than one color crayon prior to melting?
- How could you simulate how sedimentary rocks are made using crayon shavings?
- How are melted crayons similar to rocks and minerals in the earth's mantle?

CHAPTER FOUR

AIR AND SKY
Our Breath and View of the Heavens

For great is your love, higher than the heavens; your faithfulness reaches to the skies. Be exalted, O God, above the heavens; let your glory be over all the earth.

PSALM 108:4–5 (NIV)

The sky is pretty cool. It conducts electricity (lightning), changes color (blue, red-orange, and even black at night), and puts on incredible light shows near the poles (the auroras). The sky is like God's canvas, and the paintings He creates show His power and love for all creatures, including you and me.

When we look up on a clear night, every star we see is part of our galaxy. In places where city lights don't outshine the stars, the sky is clear enough to see the Milky Way and Andromeda galaxies. When astronauts look down on Earth from space at night—when the sun is on the far side of the planet—they see groups of lights, almost like stars, spread across cities and towns across Earth's surface. We live in an incredible time of technology and space

exploration that allows us to see and explore what the Bible called "the heavens." The sky above us is big and beautiful. Just think about times when you've stargazed, watched storms roll in, and seen the sun come up and go down. The air and sky are worth considering and protecting.

The Harmful Effects of Pollution

Unfortunately, because of the things humans have made (light bulbs, gas-powered engines, coal-burning power plants, and others), we've hurt the visibility of the sky and the quality of the air we breathe. These things are called **light pollution** (too much light) and **air pollution** (bad air quality).

Lightning can and does strike the same place all the time, especially if that place is tall and there's not much else around it. For example, according to their website, the Empire State Building in New York is struck about twenty-five times per year!

Light Pollution

When humans figured out how to turn electricity into light instead of relying on fire, it was a remarkable achievement. It advanced medicine, improved safety at night, and brightened our homes. Unfortunately, it also introduced light pollution, an overflow of artificial light that blocks our view of the night sky. Light pollution can also change our sleeping habits, trick animals into hibernating and eating at the wrong times, and mess with bird migrations.[1]

But light pollution isn't just a nighttime problem. During the day, haze makes it harder to see well in cities, scenic areas, and national parks. Haze forms when light hits particles of pollution in the air, clouding out what we see by lessening clarity and color.[2] Haze is like putting a pair of dirty glasses on everyone. Maybe you've seen haze or smog before. Pretty sad, isn't it? This decreased visibility wasn't part of the original design of the skies.

Air Pollution

Earth's atmosphere acts as a protective shield, blocking harmful UV sunrays and disintegrating meteors while providing breathable air for all living things. It's like a bubble of air that lets good things through and keeps bad things out. The atmosphere is made up of life-sustaining gases: 78 percent nitrogen and 21 percent oxygen, with smaller amounts of carbon dioxide, helium, and neon. Air pollution happens when the amount of these gases gets messed up or if toxic elements are added to the mix. Pollution is really bad for ecosystems and human health!

One of the most common and problematic types of air pollution is **particulate matter**, which is a mixture of solid particles and air droplets light enough to float in the air. This includes dust, pollen, soot, or smoke, but the more troubling varieties are made up of chemicals from power plants and automobiles. Air that's polluted with particulate matter is sometimes called smog. What makes it so dangerous is that these solid particles and chemicals are easy for us to breathe in and can get into our lungs. Other serious kinds of air pollution come from nitrous dioxide, sulfur dioxide, and ozone. Even carbon dioxide, which is a side effect of breathing, is considered an air pollutant when its levels go too far beyond its natural limits, since it can cause problems with ecosystems and climate systems.

Most air pollution comes from transportation, followed by power plants, industrial furnaces, brick kilns, agriculture, and unregulated burning of waste like plastics and batteries.[3] Cookstoves are unsafe sources of air pollution in many rural homes.

Think breathing in dirty air can cause health problems? You'd be right! Air pollution can hurt our lungs, brain, and heart health. Particulate matter is really bad for pregnant women and their babies. It's also linked to dementia[4] and lung cancer.[5] Together, outdoor and household air pollution lead to around seven million people dying earlier than they should every year.[6]

The sad truth is that poor air quality affects most of the world's population, according to the guidelines of the World Health Organization.[7] People living in countries where folks don't have as much money are more severely affected by air pollution,[8] and areas around big cities are particularly likely to experience dangerous levels of smog.

Today, people of color often suffer the most from air pollution and

What does the air look like—or smell like or taste like—where you live? How could you improve the air quality?

the illnesses and deaths that go along with it.[9] Since you'll find the highest air pollution in big cities with factories, it affects the people there the most—specifically the racial minorities who are more likely to live there because of outdated and unfair housing laws.* Also, homes near polluting power plants and busy roads are cheaper, so families who can't afford to live anywhere else experience higher levels of air pollution.

Want to support life? Want to make things fairer for people of all races? Fighting for clean air can help!

Meet Karl/Karla, San Francisco's Fog

The city of San Francisco is home to cable cars, the Golden Gate Bridge, and fog. In fact, it is known by some as Fog City. And back in 2010, that fog got a name when an anonymous person went on Twitter and created an account for "Karl the Fog."

Karl was pretty great, but when the person who created the account stopped posting for a while, Karla the Fog took over.

Fog is basically a cloud that hangs close to the ground. San Francisco's location—next to the ocean, where winds blow cool air toward the mainland—makes it the perfect place for fog to

---

* To learn more about how race has affected where people live, check out *How to Fight Racism Young Reader's Edition* by Jemar Tisby.

naturally occur. It's like nature's air conditioning, but it comes at a price. The cooler temperatures that moderate what might otherwise be hot summer days can make it hard for residents to see. Sometimes, the summer months themselves earn nicknames like "May Gray," "June Gloom," "No Sky July," and "Fogust."

What's the difference between fog and smog? While both can block visibility, fog is a naturally occurring weather pattern that can bring water to ecosystems where it would otherwise be scarce, while smog infuses that water with chemicals and particulate matter that causes pollution. Smog, in fact, is just a mash-up of the words *smoke* and *fog*.

Unfortunately, Karl/Karla has been making shorter appearances. According to research published in 2010, summertime fog hours in the Bay Area around San Francisco have gone down by 33 percent over the past hundred years.[11] Scientists are studying how these changes in fog levels are affecting the ecosystems in the region, as well as whether these changes are happening due to natural forces or man-made climate changes.

MONGOLIA AIR CRISIS

In 2018, Mongolia had a public health crisis when its capital city, Ulaanbaatar, reached air pollution levels more than one hundred times the acceptable limit. Tons of people (in fact, half of the country's population) had moved to the city, since it was the only place with available jobs.[12] This population growth meant a major increase in the amount of cookstoves heating homes. What did these cookstoves burn? The only affordable option people could find: coal.

The situation became so awful in Mongolia that children,

whose lungs were still developing, were in and out of the intensive care ward at hospitals. Many suffered from coughing and pneumonia. The cityscape was continually covered in a cloud of smog. But because the city was where the jobs were, many families couldn't move away.

THE CLEAN AIR ACT

In the US before 1970, cities across the country were disappearing behind clouds of thick smog. The **Clean Air Act** allowed the government to regulate air pollution emissions from sources like vehicles, power plants, and factories. It also addressed chemical pollutants that were damaging the atmosphere's ozone layer, which protects us from harmful UV rays from the sun, and aimed to reduce acid rain and improve air quality and visibility.

Our Responsibility

We may not be able to remove all light and air pollution—and as the population of the planet grows, we'll have more challenges with air quality and visibility—but we can still do a lot to limit and reverse the damage. It's time to support the solutions that keep our air cleaner and safer. With all the technological advances in energy options, we can keep the air cleaner for everyone. Clean, breathable air should be available to all. God has trusted us with the air, sky, and heavens. We have a responsibility to take care of and protect this priceless gift.

How well can you see the stars from your home? What are some ways you could limit light pollution in your neighborhood?

A Biblical Perspective

God sees every part of the planet that has gone wrong and is broken, including things like air and light pollution. And He gives us mercy for our faults and failures in messing up His creation. In John 3:16, where it famously says, "For God so loved *the world*, that he gave his only Son" (emphasis added), the Greek word the verse uses, *kosmos*, is for the entire universe. This means that God gave His Son not only to redeem you and me but the whole universe as well. Do you love the world the way God does? Will you care for it as part of its redemption?

God's Creativity on Display

What do you think we can learn about God from looking at the sky? Psalm 19:1 says, "The heavens declare the glory of God, and the sky above proclaims his handiwork." We know that God is glorious, and we know that He's shared a bit of that glory with us by allowing us to see the awesome things He's made. We need to

let the glory of God's natural lights in the sky reach more areas of our world. Clean air and clear views of the sky help others see God's glory in creation. By doing your part against air and light pollution, you're making it possible for present and future kids to be amazed by a starry sky and wonder about the Maker of the cosmos.

God Is for Us

The skies and heavens aren't only beautiful—they're also perfectly planned, and they show us that God is in control. The types of gases and the way they're mixed in our atmosphere are just right for life to prosper. Compared with all the other planets in the galaxy, Earth's atmosphere is a perfect fit for the life it sustains, as humans and plants share oxygen and carbon dioxide to live and breathe.

Outside the Milky Way, billions of other galaxies travel through the universe as it expands. The Hubble Space Telescope clocked one galaxy moving three million miles per hour away from us. Christians believe that God set everything spinning, and all of it—the expansion of the universe, the spin of galaxies, and the way our planet revolves around the sun—happens by God's direction, meaning by His established natural laws, like gravity.

In Psalm 46:10, God tells us to "be still, and know that I am God" (NIV). This verse makes us stop and think about who's in control, and who positioned Earth at just the right distance from the sun so the planet wouldn't burn up or freeze over. The God of the heavens and the Milky Way, the God who made Earth perfect for you and me to live—do you trust Him? Yes, humans have caused some problems with the planet and each other, but God invites us to bring our concerns and our brokenness to Him in prayer. Look up on a sunny day or during a starry night and think about your place on this earth. Ask God for direction on how to play your part in solving environmental problems like air pollution.

HOW YOU CAN MAKE A DIFFERENCE

MAKE TIME TO APPRECIATE THE NIGHTTIME SKY

When we appreciate the sky above us, we feel more connected to God's creation. And feeling connected to creation gives us more reasons to take care of it!

Enjoy stargazing and astronomical views

- Check out NASA's "Astronomy Picture of the Day" (http://apod.nasa.gov) for awesome photos and videos of the cosmos. As you look through the galaxies, nebula, stars, planets, and other space sights, take a moment and tell God how awesome and creative He is for making such amazing things!
- Learn more about space at the NASA Space Place (http://spaceplace.nasa.gov), which is full of crafts, activities, and educational tidbits.
- Look up Dark Sky parks in your area to see where you can enjoy the stars in their awesome splendor (on clear nights, of course).

IMPROVE AIR QUALITY

We can work with nature's God-designed ways of cleaning the air! How? Plant a tree!

- Trees are natural air filters, removing air pollutants like sulfur dioxide, ozone, nitrogen oxides, and other hard-to-pronounce things. They also clean up the particulates that make smog out of fog.

REDUCE LIGHT POLLUTION AND HAZE

Turning off lights at night doesn't just limit your electricity use, it improves our view of the nighttime sky and prevents confusion for migrating birds.

Switch it off

- Keep your lights off whenever possible to help reduce light pollution, save on your energy bill, and reduce your carbon footprint. That's a trifecta of awesomeness!
- Switch to LED lighting. LED light bulbs are bright enough to read by, but not so bright they mess with nature's natural beauty. They also take less energy than other light bulbs.

RESEARCH CLEANER POWER SOURCES

Many of our everyday activities affect the air we breathe. About 60 percent of the US's electricity comes from power plants that burn fossil fuels like coal and natural gas. Less than 20 percent comes from renewable power sources like wind, hydropower, and solar.[13] In addition to using less electricity, you should check out how renewable power sources work and why we should be using them more.

Get to Know William Kamkwamba

- When William Kamkwamba was fourteen years old, his home in Malawi—a country in East Africa—went through a terrible famine. William had to drop out of school, but he never stopped learning. He studied electronics at his local library and figured out how to build a wind turbine after seeing a picture of one in a US junior high textbook called *Using Energy*. William's first wind turbine—made from spare parts and scrap recovered from a junkyard—powered some electronics in his family's home.

- Read William's story in his book, *The Boy Who Harnessed the Wind*, or watch the movie that was based on the book.

Start a STEM club

- Head to your local library and learn more about the technology you use every day. Many libraries and schools even have STEM (Science, Technology, Engineering, and Math) programs designed for kids your age.
- Here are a few things you could learn about:

  ★ Dynamos! How do generators make electricity? How could you power a dynamo without using fossil fuels?
  ★ Wind Turbines! The higher a turbine is off the ground, the more consistent the wind flow tends to be. But building a tower stable enough for the attached wind turbine can be a challenge. Which building techniques make the strongest towers? How tall could you build a tower using household objects?

★ Hydroelectric Dams! About 7 percent of the US's electric power is generated by waterpower, but how do they work? How have people used waterpower in the past? What could you power with it today?

SUPPORT NONPROFITS WORKING TO DECREASE AIR POLLUTION

◊ **Earthjustice** is a nonprofit law organization that works to protect public health from air pollution and to fight for clean energy solutions.

◊ **Moving Windmills** is William Kamkwamba's nonprofit, which is working to help the youth of Malawi learn STEM skills so they can use creative problem solving to tackle the issues facing their country.

CHAPTER FIVE

WOODLANDS
Our Disappearing Forests

The earth brought forth vegetation, plants yielding seed according to their own kinds, and trees bearing fruit in which is their seed, each according to its kind. And God saw that it was good.

GENESIS 1:12

Did you know that the world has more than sixty thousand different kinds of trees? And every one of them is made for the climate where it lives. Some trees have leaves shaped like ovals. Others have heart-shaped leaves. Still others have spiked or lobed (like the bottom of an ear) shapes.

Some are shaped like broccoli while others look like umbrellas. God designed each leaf to be able to capture sunlight and hold on to water in the best way possible for where the tree grows. Leaves on tall trees tend to be tiny and leaves on trees that are lower to ground tend to be bigger. There are so many different kinds of leaves out there! And let's not even get into conifers.

Just kidding, let's get into conifers!

These amazing trees have needles for leaves and they grow cones (can you guess where conifers got their names?), and many are shaped like a cone with their longest branches at the bottom. When most people think about conifers, they imagine Christmas trees (which are conifers) and cold weather, but conifers are found in all kinds of climates and ecosystems. Plus, they hold some cool world records. The tallest tree, the oldest tree, and the biggest tree are all conifers (and they're all found in California).[1] While conifers only represent about 1 percent of the different species of trees in the world, they are found all over the globe and provide for almost half of the lumber (and paper) needs in the world!

Let's not forget about the rainforests though. A rainforest's humid setting makes it the perfect place to find lots of exotic plant life. Big, beautiful flowers draw in colorful hummingbirds and butterflies. Venus flytraps snap their jaws on insect prey. Green

Methuselah, a bristlecone pine in California's White Mountains, is the world's oldest living tree at more than 4,850 years old. The previous record holder, Prometheus—another bristlecone pine— was killed when a scientist attempted to measure how old it was (it was at least 4,862 years old when it died).

plants of all kinds—some with leaves as big as kites!—can be found in rainforests.

But it isn't just the plants that are cool. Rainforests are home to some amazing animals too! Jaguars climb trees to stalk their prey or rest on a bough. Monkeys scale the towering trunks and swing from branches and vines. The forest is bursting with life. It's a playground for God's most raucous and curious creatures on the planet. And it's disappearing at an alarming rate.

Deforestation

As the world's population continues to grow, we use and destroy more and more forests to meet our needs for food, stuff, and space for homes and buildings. This is known as **deforestation**, when forests disappear because we don't replant trees fast enough to replace them. Humans have wiped out more than 30 percent of all the planet's forests in the last few hundred years.[2]

It isn't that we can't cut down trees. When foresters—people

who cut down trees as their job—are careful about which trees they cut down and make sure they plant new ones to replace them, forests can actually get healthier. How? Because forests are healthiest when they have lots of different kinds of trees: big trees, little trees, old trees, young trees.[3]

Unfortunately, many trees are illegally cut down in ways that mess up entire forest areas for years and years. And tropical rainforests are especially in danger. In 2019, a football field's worth of rainforest trees were lost every six seconds.[4]

Why do you think forests are healthiest when they have different kinds of trees? How is that like a community of people?

One major way rainforests are disappearing is by something called *slash-and-burn agriculture*. It's basically what it sounds like. Farmers cut down (slash) forests to make room for their crops, then burn the trees because the ashes make good fertilizer. But after a few years, the once-fertile land uses up the available nutrients and it stops growing crops. The farm is abandoned, and the farmer cuts down more trees elsewhere to start the process all over. Where is this happening? Unfortunately, all over the place. Forests are commonly cleared by fire in Southeast Asia, tropical Africa, and North and South America.

So why can't we just pass a law banning slash-and-burn agriculture? It's complicated. Although the practice is bad for forests, it makes money for the farmers who are doing it, many of whom don't have any other ways to make money. Globally, one in four people rely on forests to make a living.[5] And around 750 million people live in forests.[6]

The Carbon Cycle

One of the reasons deforestation is so bad for the environment is because it throws off the balance of the carbon cycle. Carbon is an amazing element. When God created the world, He used carbon

The Forest Carbon Cycle

CO$_2$ IN ATMOSPHERE

COMBUSTION OF FUELS

Industry

Fossil fuels
(oil, gas, coal)

DIFFUSION

CELL RESPIRATION

Plants

Animals

DISSOLVED CO$_2$

BICARBONATES

**CARBONATES
IN SEDIMENTS**

DECOMPOSERS:
Animals, plants, algae

as one of the main building blocks for all living things. We can't have life without carbon. But carbon must work in a balance with the rest of creation in order for life to continue.

Most of the world's carbon is locked up in rocks underground—coal is a rock mainly made of carbon. But when we burn coal for fuel, it is released into the atmosphere. The carbon in the atmosphere acts like a house's thermostat. When carbon dioxide (the gaseous version of carbon) is at a healthy level, it keeps temperatures stable and the weather predictable. But as more carbon gets added to the atmosphere, the thermostat goes up, the temperatures get warmer, and the weather gets more unpredictable. We need to rebalance the system to get back to more stable climate patterns. How? With plants!

The Importance of the Rainforests

While all forests are important—as homes for animals and people, as sources for building materials and paper, and as great places to store carbon so it isn't overwhelming our atmosphere—rainforests are especially precious to the planet. Why? Because they house more biodiversity within their borders than any other area on earth. The Amazon rainforest is home to more than six thousand different types of trees,[7] which provide cozy homes for several million species of animals and other life-forms.[8] It is the largest remaining portion of

The carbon cycle goes like this: carbon moves from the air to plants (in photosynthesis), from plants to animals, from plants and animals to soil (through decomposition), from living things and fossil fuels to the atmosphere, and from the atmosphere to the ocean.

The Amazon is home to some of the most unique animals on the planet: black spider monkeys, pink river dolphins, spotted jaguars, poison dart frogs, and many people's favorite, sloths. In fact, one out of every ten known animal species is found there, with over two thousand new species of plants and animals being discovered since 1999.[10]

humid tropical forest; nearly two-thirds of it is in Brazil. However, in the past fifty years, we've lost about 17 percent of the Amazonian rainforest, mostly due to forest clearing for cattle ranching.[9]

We can't afford to keep cutting down forests without planting new trees to take their place. Clearing forests reduces humidity and rainfall, which farmers rely on, especially in places like Brazil. If the deforestation continues and we lose 40 percent of the trees, the Amazon rainforest could become the Amazon savannah (a completely different kind of ecosystem).[11] At the rate things are going, this could happen in less than thirty years.[12]

Our rainforests help regulate our global climate and help farmers around the world grow the food we eat. Removing huge areas of natural forests is similar to cutting off a body's connection to a vital organ like a lung; it throws off the whole system.

A Way Forward

A healthy planet needs thriving forests. Replanting forests and making current forests healthier will help with air pollution, climate regulation, water quality, and more.

We can start using foresting techniques that are less harmful to the earth and allow for trees to grow back successfully and forests to recover, while at the same time considering the jobs of people who live there, like farmers and foresters. Our forests clean our air, filter our water, regulate the life-generating carbon cycle, provide food and medicines, strengthen our soil, and provide shelter for a wonderful abundance of plants and animals. This, along with their natural beauty, makes them a valuable part of God's creation!

A Biblical Perspective

Trees play a big part in the Bible. According to Genesis, the first book in the Bible, God created trees and said *it is good*. Later, Adam and Eve were created to live in a garden surrounded by trees.

One of these trees was called the tree of the knowledge of good and evil. Another was called the tree of life. The first one was off limits to Adam and Eve, but they ate from it anyway, and creation has never been the same since. The second tree became off limits after they

No one knows what the fruit from the tree of the knowledge of good and evil looked like. It is popular to show it as an apple, but it could have been any kind of fruit—maybe even one of your favorites. What do you think made the forbidden fruit so tempting?

disobeyed God. He knew that mankind wasn't ready for the tree of life while there was sin in the world.

The tree of life makes another appearance in the book of Revelation. The new heaven and new earth have come, and "in the middle of the street, and on either side of the river, was the tree of life, which bore twelve fruits, each tree yielding its fruit every month. The leaves of the tree were for the healing of the nations" (Revelation 22:2 NKJV). It's a place where heaven and earth are in harmony again, and God gives nourishment to the entire world through a tree.[13]

This tells us that God uses all of creation, but especially trees, to show His justice and mercy to people through all time. Our God had a plan for people and the tree of life from the beginning of history.

God's Plan for Trees

Did you know that trees praise God too, in their own treelike way? Isaiah 44:23 tells every tree in the forest to "break forth into singing" because the Lord has redeemed His people. "For you shall go out in joy and be led forth in peace; the mountains and the hills before you shall break forth into singing, and all the trees of the field shall clap their hands" (Isaiah 55:12).

Jesus and Trees

Have you ever thought about the fact that, before His ministry began at age thirty, Jesus worked with the same type of wooden material that would make up the cross? He sawed, sanded, whittled, and carved slabs of tree. He would've hammered and nailed pieces together. The feel of wood was very familiar to Him in life, and it's what He'd voluntarily lean back against during His death. All along, Jesus, as God, knew that He would one day use the timber material of His earthly career to bring about our great salvation. What a humble Savior, worthy of our worship! He interacted with nature and trees in a meaningful way—in both life and in death—to serve others.

How can you interact with nature and trees in a meaningful way like Jesus did? How can you make your branch of God's kingdom a welcoming place for people to flock to?

Jesus came to earth and claimed to be the source of eternal life, the true vine with many branches (John 15:5). In fact, He compared the kingdom to a large tree that grows and spreads out "so that the birds of the air come and make nests in its branches" (Matthew 13:32).

HOW YOU CAN MAKE A DIFFERENCE

LEARN ABOUT AND ENGAGE WITH YOUR LOCAL FORESTS

The best way to learn about the value of forests is to get to know the ones in your area. Experiencing your nearby forests will help you give thanks for these important habitats.

Find a tree field guide

- Leaf forms, bark types, and other features offer clues that help us tell which tree is which. A field guide has pictures and illustrations of each tree species and their unique attributes.

If you or a caregiver has a smartphone, you can check out the iNaturalist app to help identify trees as well.

🍂 Take a field guide or smartphone with you to a forest or your backyard and compare the different features of each tree.

Join local restoration or tree-planting projects

🍂 Look up what other people are doing in your area to protect the health of your forests. There may be tree planting events or invasive species removal projects. The Nature Conservancy is a good place to start.

Check out Global Forest Watch online

🍂 This online forest monitoring system led by the World Resources Institute uses satellite imagery to see changes in tree cover in near–real time around the planet.

ENSURE YOUR RAINFOREST PRODUCTS ARE SOURCED FROM ETHICAL SUPPLY CHAINS

Slash-and-burn deforestation and other unsustainable farming methods make up nearly 80 percent of deforestation in tropical and subtropical areas.[14] You can help by using your money or asking your caregivers to support farmers who are using earth-friendly farming techniques.

Cocoa

Cocoa grows well under a forest canopy, but many cocoa farmers are cutting down forests to grow a greater amount in the sun. This messes up soil, wipes out wildlife habitat, and creates more chemical runoff that pollutes streams and waterways.[15]

◊ Look for chocolate certified by the Rainforest Alliance, which partners with small-scale cocoa farmers to encourage returning to shade-grown cocoa. Let's make sure the chocolate we eat doesn't leave a bad taste in our mouth because of how it is grown!

Make Daily Choices that Conserve Wood Products

From school assignments to drawing for fun, you use paper all the time! Did you know that the paper you choose and buy can lessen unnecessary and unsustainable deforestation?

Make informed decisions

◊ Choose products that come from sustainable harvesting practices, which replant and restore forests in the process.

◊ Purchase products that display certifications from groups like the Forest Stewardship Council (FSC) and the Sustainable Forestry Initiative (SFI).

◊ Conserve the amount of paper you use and reuse it when you can. Avoid one-time-use paper products such as paper plates and cups.

◊ Always recycle your paper. In the US, about 68 percent of the paper and paperboard product we use each year is recycled, while the rest—17.2 million tons—ends up in landfills.[16]

◊ Purchase paper made from recycled materials when it's an option.

Check Out These Groups Who Are Working to Reverse Deforestation

- **Plant with Purpose** works with communities to reverse deforestation through tree planting projects around the world.
- **Amazon Watch** has been working for decades to protect the rainforest and the many different people groups who live in the Amazon Basin.

CHAPTER SIX

SOIL

Agriculture's Active Ingredient

"Unless a kernel of wheat falls to the ground and dies, it remains only a single seed. But if it dies, it produces many seeds."

JOHN 12:24 (NIV)

How often do you think about where your food comes from, or the soil that helped it grow? Farms are living ecosystems—full of plants, animals, soil, water, and air working together in a balance that keeps the land growing food for years and years. To have the biggest harvests of the food we eat, farms need to have a well-balanced natural system. And a key ingredient to a farm's health is its soil.

Did you know that a single teaspoon of soil is alive with billions of teeny-tiny organisms? "Living soil" is one of the main reasons farms can grow (and keep growing) food. The little organisms living in the soil do a lot of hard work! They break down nutrients for plants, build soil structure, and improve water absorption.

SOIL VS. DIRT

What's the difference between dirt and soil? Dirt is made from rocks that break down over time, as wind and water slowly transform rocks into sand, clay, and silt. Soil is dirt plus water, air, and bits of old plants and animals (organic matter). Mushrooms, slime molds, fungi, and bacteria in the soil all work to help break down dead things and release their nutrients for reuse. These natural fertilizers are the champions of soil health!

Unfortunately, we have seriously messed up earth's soil by overfarming the land and not giving it time to recover.

Have you ever run so hard you get a pain in your side? It takes a few minutes of rest before you can start running again. Agricultural soil is similar in that it can also "wear out." The land needs a chance to rest and rebuild its nutrients naturally. When it doesn't get rest, the land suffers and can't grow food as well. The United Nations (UN) guesses that twenty-four billion tons of fertile soil is lost each year.[1]

Unsustainable Agricultural Practices

In the past fifty years, farming has changed a lot to keep up with the growing population. Small family farms have given way to farms owned and worked by big companies, which is known as **industrial agriculture**.

Industrial agriculture is large-scale and uses technology to grow the most food per square foot possible with crops (like rice, corn, and wheat) and livestock (like chicken, cows, and pigs). These types of farms typically only produce one type of crop instead of lots of different ones. And to make sure the crops grow well and don't get eaten by bugs, industrial farms tend to use a lot of chemical fertilizers and pesticides.

Meat production happens in **confined animal feeding operations (CAFO)**, where the livestock live in cramped conditions. If that doesn't sound very comfortable, it isn't. Worse still, by living so close together, these animals are especially susceptible to the spread of disease. To keep them healthy, farmers give the animals lots of vaccines and antibiotics. Unfortunately, that also leads to a rise in germs that are better at resisting the vaccines and antibiotics.

So why do companies use these methods? To make sure they can make the most food possible to feed the most people possible . . . and to make the most money possible.

And these methods—industrial agriculture and CAFO—do grow a lot of food. But there's a price, and the environment can't keep paying it forever. Growing the same crops year after year can strip the land of its biodiversity and the natural ways of staying useful for growing crops. Eventually, the soil washes away or turns into plain old dirt in a process called **soil erosion**. Around the planet, soil is eroded ten to forty times faster than it's replaced, leading to a loss of cropland that's close to the size of Iceland every year.[2]

What are your favorite foods to eat? How do you think those foods affect the environment?

And it isn't just the land that suffers because of soil erosion. To make up for the loss of soil, farms end up using more chemical fertilizers. But these fertilizers don't stay on the plants, often getting washed away and ending up in rivers and oceans. This fertilizer causes an overgrowth of algae, creating "dead zones" where oxygen runs out and fish suffocate. Many bodies of water around the world, like the Baltic Sea and Chesapeake Bay, suffer from dead zones, harming fish harvests and affecting fishing communities.

The Food and Waste Problem

Unhealthy soil is one problem; food shortage is another. The planet produces an abundance of food, yet between 720 and 811 million people went hungry in 2020.[3] In the same year, nearly a quarter of children under five years of age didn't grow as much as they should have because they lacked the vitamins and minerals needed for a healthy diet (known as malnutrition).[4] Farmers produce enough food to feed around 10 billion people, which is 1.5 times the global population.[5] However, we waste about a third of it.[6]

Imagine throwing out a third of your birthday presents or letting a third of the food in your refrigerator go bad. Food waste is a serious global problem. It's not about having enough food for everyone; rather, it's about getting nutritious food to everyone who needs it.

Global Food Production and Waste

$1 TRILLION DOLLARS' WORTH OF FOOD IS LOST OR WASTED EVERY YEAR.

IF EVEN 25% OF THE FOOD CURRENTLY LOST OR WASTED COULD BE SAVED, IT COULD EASILY FEED 870 MILLION HUNGRY PEOPLE IN THE WORLD.

UNITED STATES

In the United States alone, $48.3 billion is thrown away each year. Overall losses are $90–100 billion per year.

EUROPE

The food currently wasted in Europe—about 6.7 million tonnes—could feed 200 million people.

ASIA

In Asia, around 23 million tonnes of food cereals, 12 million tonnes of fruits, and 21 million tonnes of vegetables are lost each year.

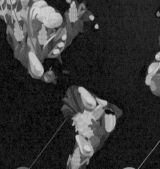

LATIN AMERICA

In Latin America the food lost or wasted could feed 300 million people.

AFRICA

In Africa, losses can reach up to 50% for some less hardy crops, such as fruits, vegetables, and root crops.

INDIA

An estimated 580 billion rupees (nearly $8 billion) is wasted each year in India, in agricultural produce.

AUSTRALIA

In Australia, an estimated $10.5 billion was spent on items thrown away (more than $5,000 per capita per year).

Sustainable Agriculture

The problems of too little soil and too much food waste for a growing population can be solved in part with sustainable agriculture. This includes farming methods that allow us to grow crops and tend livestock without hurting the land's ability to continue to grow more food for our future needs. We are learning how to work with nature to keep the soil healthy and the land fertile and productive on our farms and in community and home gardens.

Our challenges for the future are to match how we grow and eat food with farming practices that support healthy soil, as well as getting the food to everyone in society. We need to rely less on farms that grow single crops like wheat, corn, and grain (most of which goes to feeding livestock), and focus on harvesting nutritious veggies, fruits, and beans more locally when possible. Using too many fertilizers and pesticides can really mess up the soil and water, so we should do less of that too.

A Way Forward

How can we balance the needs to protect our soil and feed the earth's population? This will take creativity from leaders and people around the world, but it's not out of reach. The good news for you and me is that there are small things we can do right now to both protect our land and provide for our neighbors, like choosing food that's grown sustainably. For once, it's a *good* excuse for you to be picky at the dinner table!

A Biblical Perspective

As Christians, we should try to live like Jesus taught his disciples and give generously. This might mean sending and serving food to those in need, like in homeless shelters. It may mean growing healthy fruits and vegetables in a community garden. Or it could mean supporting farms that are doing a good job caring for the land, its soil, and, in turn, its people. It's almost like we've been given back the gardening tools from the garden of Eden: God's presence and practical insights into how the world was meant to be. God gave us the example of Eden to inspire us with ways we can care for the earth.

Made from Dirt and Made to Care for It

As it says in Genesis, God made the first person out of dirt, but humans were also made in the image of God. We are connected both to the earth and to heaven. After Adam and Eve sinned by eating the fruit God told them not to, humans experienced a broken relationship with the soil for the very first time (Genesis 3:19). But God commanded us to work the land, and even now we're still charged with its care. When we admit to God the ways we've been selfish and humbly ask for His forgiveness and help in changing our ways, God promises to hear us and heal the land (2 Chronicles 7:14). When we care for the earth, we are taking part in God's original design for us. We can walk with God where we live and honor Him in how we care for the earth.

God's Redemption Plan for Soil

In nature, we constantly see death producing life. When living stuff dies, it decays—breaks down—into natural fertilizer. This **decaying material** at the bottom of the **food chain** turns into life's new beginnings. This circle of life starts and ends with soil. When we disrespect the land and don't honor its limits, we can strip it of nutrients and steal away its ability to grow more plants. Honestly, it's kind of scary, because when this happens, it hurts people all over the world.

But as Christians, we know that God can make dead things alive again. The Lord says: "Behold, I am making all things new" (Revelation 21:5). "*All* things" includes the land we live on and the soil we need. When we learn to love and respect the earth the way God does, and we understand His plans to make every broken bit of it new again, our love for both God and nature grows like a plant in good soil. He is good and faithful—*even to dirt!*

A Calling to Feed the Hungry

Jesus cared a lot about people's need for food while He walked on the earth. He had compassion on a crowd of five thousand people and miraculously fed them with a small amount of fish and bread. Scripture tells us in 1 John that if we have the world's goods and see a brother or sister in need but don't make the effort to help them, then we lie and don't practice the truth (3:17).

God uses His people to do His work, especially when it comes to taking care of those who are in need. In Acts 11:29, the disciples sent food to other Christians living in Judea to support them through a famine. We can follow their example today! When our Christian brothers and sisters around the world and at home need more food sources—whether due to  famine, food shortage, or natural disaster—it's our responsibility as followers of Jesus to figure out how to cultivate the earth and get food to every hungry person.

HOW YOU CAN MAKE A DIFFERENCE

UNDERSTAND WHAT *ORGANIC* AND *LOCAL* MEAN

We're often encouraged to buy food that's better for the environment and people, but food labels can be confusing. It's helpful to know what to look for.

Organic

- For food to be labeled and certified as organic, it must follow some pretty specific rules, which include the soil and water quality where it grew, animal-raising practices, pest and weed control, and restrictions on chemical additives. Food that is labeled "organic" is probably the best thing you can buy to help the environment.

Local

- At local farmers markets, you can ask about the farmers' organic practices. Because it costs farmers money to get their food labeled as organic, some may be doing the right things without getting credit for it.

- Local food also doesn't need to travel as far to get from the farm to your table. That means fewer trucks on the roads putting carbon into the atmosphere.

PREVENT FOOD WASTE

Every year, Americans throw out nearly 80 billion pounds of food. It comes out to about 219 pounds of waste per person and nearly 40 percent of the US food supply.[7] By making changes to our buying and eating habits, we can better appreciate the gift of food.

Understand expiration labels

- "Best if used by" means that food may not be quite as tasty after the date, but it is still safe to eat. "Use by" is for foods that have a time limit for food safety.[8] Don't eat bad food that is actually expired, but don't throw good food away.

Compost

- Compost works wonders for soil health in your home garden, as mulch in your yard, and/or for houseplants.
- What can be composted: fruits and vegetables, eggshells,

coffee grounds and filters, tea bags, nut shells, shredded newspaper, cardboard, paper, yard trimmings, grass clippings, houseplants, hay and straw, leaves, sawdust, wood chips, cotton and wool rags, hair and fur.[9]

- What can't be composted: diseased plants, dog or cat poo, coal or charcoal ash, dairy products (such as butter, milk, sour cream, yogurt) and eggs (except eggshells), fats, grease, lard or oils, meat or fish bones and scraps, black walnut tree leaves or twigs, or yard trimmings treated with chemical pesticides.[10]

- One trick to make sure your compost doesn't stink up the house is to store compost items in a bag in the freezer until you can add them to your outdoor pile.

Freeze or repurpose food

- Save foods like meat and bread before their expiration date comes up by freezing them for later.

- Freeze extra fruit, spinach, or kale and use it to make smoothies later. Turn your vegetables into stock or juice them. Be proactive and creative!

- Learn how to make fruit jam, how to pickle, or how to store vegetables in jars.

- Use stale bread to make French toast or homemade croutons for tasty salads!

Welcome imperfect produce

- There are programs that sell produce with discoloring, bumps, or irregular shapes (which supermarkets often throw out even though it's still edible and tasty). Look into Imperfect Foods and Misfits Market.

VISIT A FARM USING THE RIGHT PRACTICES

If land is overused, soil loses the necessary ingredients for life. We can pack soil with chemical fertilizers to make up for it, but the microbes and fungi in healthy soil aren't replaceable. Farms that are doing the right things—growing more than one kind of food, not relying on chemical fertilizers, using natural methods to grow their produce and animals—are worth a visit!

Learn about a farm's unique journey to sustainability

- There's not a single plan that works for every farm, but depending on each one's location and climate, sustainable techniques can (and should!) be used.
- Visit farms near you to learn about their earth-friendly practices. Be sure to ask about growing different grains and veggies, rotating crops, planting cover crops, no-till or reduced-till methods, livestock integration, agroforestry, and buffer zones. If these words are confusing, just write them down and ask a farmer to explain them to you!

SUPPORT LOCAL AND INTERNATIONAL ORGANIZATIONS

Learn about food issues in your area and look for ways to help communities get food in ways that keep their lands productive.

Volunteer or start a food charity effort at church

- Churches often have or support food programs like soup kitchens or food pantries. Get your family to volunteer at one or start one in your local area.

Plant a neighborhood garden

- Reach out to your neighbors to see if there's interest in growing food together (or ask your school!). You might be surprised at the skills your neighbors have (green thumbs, carpenters, etc.).
- Decide on a site. If it's not in someone's yard, you will probably need to ask for permission from whoever owns the property. You may even have to get permission from your local government. That's okay. Get a grown-up to help you figure things out. If it is important to you, you can find a way.
- Research crops that do well in your local climate and design your garden. Share your produce with neighbors or donate part of the harvest to a food pantry.

Support organizations

- **Growing Hope Globally** is a faith-based nonprofit that works on food insecurity issues alongside churches and communities to end world hunger.
- **Echo: Hope Against Hunger** is a faith-based organization that helps small-scale farmers and their families learn to use sustainable agricultural practices.
- See what organizations are active in your area. Have a caregiver do an internet search for groups that help food-insecure people in your community. These organizations might need some help sorting food donations or packing food boxes, and many would welcome help from all ages.

CHOOSE SUSTAINABLE FASHION OVER FAST FASHION

You may not think about farms when you purchase clothing, but our fabrics contain agricultural products, like cotton, flax, or hemp. These materials require land, natural resources, and labor.

Wake up to the fast-fashion waste problem

- To meet the demand for new clothes, farms that support the fast fashion industry use fertilizers and chemicals that end up polluting rivers and streams. Plus, chemicals are still needed to dye and finish fabric.
- About 2,700 liters (around 713 gallons) of water are used to make a single T-shirt[11]—that's the same amount of water one person usually drinks in three and a half years.

Shop with sustainable fashion in mind

- Look for certification labels—such as Fair Wear Foundation, Fair Trade Certified, Ethical Trading Initiative, and Certified B Corporation—for companies that use practices that protect the people who make their products.
- Check for clothes with the chemical content certification label OEKO-TEX, GOTS, or BLUESIGN.

Wear the hand-me-downs!

- Buy secondhand clothing from thrift shops and consignment stores.
- Be sure to donate your old clothes to organizations that need them once they no longer fit.

CHAPTER SEVEN

POLLINATORS
Our Overlooked Helpers

> Now John wore a garment of camel's hair
> and a leather belt around his waist, and his
> food was locusts and wild honey.

MATTHEW 3:4

Do bees come to mind when you use a dollop of honey? How about when you bite into a crisp apple slice or carve a silly face into a pumpkin? Around 75 percent of the world's biggest agricultural crops count on **pollinators**, which makes them essential to our environment.[1] We have pollinators to thank whenever we enjoy foods like potatoes, carrots, bell peppers, squash, avocados, apples, blueberries, lemons, and many others. The fruits and seeds produced from pollination, as well as the insects themselves, make up a huge part of the diets of other animals, and without these insects, the **food web** would break down across the animal and plant kingdoms.

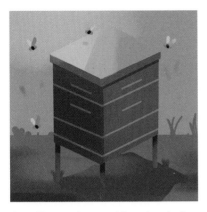

A pollinator is anything that helps carry pollen from one part of a flower, bush, or tree to another to allow that plant to produce fruits, seeds, and young plants.

Around 80 percent of all flowering plants depend on insects and other animals for pollination.[2] We wouldn't have the variety of flowers that beautify our planet without pollinators. Think of the wonders we would lose in the world without this complex, mutual "friendship" between plants and insects. Unfortunately, pollinators are in trouble. They've been dying out because of habitat loss, pesticide use, and diseases—and they need our help to recover.

The Decline of Insects

Scientists are abuzz with the fact that insect populations—including important pollinator species—are shrinking around the world. In Germany alone, flying insects in nature reserves decreased by 76 percent from 1989 to 2016.[3] More than 40 percent of insect species are threatened with extinction.[4] Findings like these have some people worried about an "insect apocalypse." If we lose our bugs, the crops that depend on pollination won't grow, and **food chains** and food webs will get seriously messed up. But as with much in nature, the future is not certain or always clear.

To make a smart guess about how insects are doing in the world, scientists sometimes study insects in one or a few areas, then assume that's how insects are doing everywhere (since that's the only data available, we have to work with what we've got!). The problem is that judging the entire insect population based on one small piece of it is like saying that all desserts taste gross because you don't like Tuna Jell-O Pie (which is a real thing that people ate decades ago). The point is that sometimes, you can't judge the whole world by one little section of it.

Even with the difficulties involved in figuring out specific population numbers, scientists have found that land-dwelling insect populations have been shrinking over time. If that trend

WHAT IS POLLINATION?

Pollination happens when pollen goes from the stamen of a plant to the stigma of either the same plant (self-pollination) or a different one (cross-pollination). When the pollen hits the stigma, the plant can produce fruits or seeds. Insects, birds, and bats can all transfer pollen, but insects are by far the most active pollinators. In fact, insects have a special relationship with plants that benefits both. Flowers catch the insects' attention with their vibrant colors and sweet-smelling, sugary nectar. Some insects have special tools and abilities to get to the pollen or nectar, like long, rolled "tongues" that uncoil and reach the nectar at the deep base of tubular flowers. The blue-banded bees of Australia, along with many carpenter bees and bumblebees, buzz and vibrate to release pollen, a fascinating trick called "buzz pollination."

continues, it'll mean trouble for all of us. If we want pollinators to keep pollinating, we need to do something to protect and support our valuable insects.

Bees

Globally, the number of different kinds of bee species is estimated at 20,000, with around 3,600 in the US and Canada alone. However, many species of bumblebees and honeybees are in trouble across North America. The rusty patched bumblebee was placed on the endangered species list not too long ago. Honeybee colonies in the US have shrunk by 3.5 million over six decades (in 1947, the record high was six million).[5] Although they receive less attention, wild bees are even more endangered. For example, over half of the native bee species disappeared in an Illinois area during the last century.[6]

Pollination is critical to our survival. Approximately 85 percent of all plants—more than 150 food crops in the US—depend on pollinators to produce seeds, which are key to forming the next generation of plants. This, in turn, provides food for the next generation of pollinators and other life. Since the plants are rooted in place, pollinators act as the agent to transfer pollen for them.

Butterflies and Moths

Butterflies and moths are also experiencing noteworthy declines. In North America, the iconic monarch butterfly used to frequently flutter about our yards. Now their orange wings outlined with black patterns and white dots are rarely seen.

Over twenty years, North American monarch

Monarch butterflies are incredible insects. Although adult butterflies only live about four to five weeks, they migrate from the northeast United States to the mountains of central Mexico each year—a distance between 1,200 and 2,800 miles!

butterfly numbers dropped to a fraction of their former glory. In the East, monarch butterflies declined by 90 percent, and in the west, they dropped by 50 percent.[7] Scientists and citizens are worried about them. A 2020 monarch count clocked in alarmingly around the estimated point of collapse[8], and in 2022, the migratory monarch was placed on the endangered species list.[9] Efforts are underway to build "monarch waystations"—stopping points with food and shelter—along their impressive three-thousand-mile migration to Mexico.

Bats

Bats are important nocturnal pollinators in tropical and desert climates. Most bat species that feed off and help pollinate flowers live in Africa, Southeast Asia, and the Pacific Islands. More than three hundred different kinds of fruits depend on bats for pollination, including mangoes, bananas, and guavas.[10] In North America, some bat species, which also eat millions of mosquitoes (thank you, bats!), are being wiped out by a fungal disease called white-nose syndrome, which shows up as white fungus on their muzzles and wings.

Our Responsibility

Though the insects and pollinators may be declining today, there's a lot we can do to help them bounce back. Because of their important role in pollination and in our ecosystems, butterflies, bats, and bees are all in need of our support and protection. They represent millions of other insects like beetles, wasps, and katydids that are also suffering significant declines in the wild. Sadly, these insects are floundering due primarily to human action and inaction. Major causes include excessive use of pesticides, increase in monoculture (growing single crops such as corn and soybeans) that limits an area's plant diversity, the rise and growth of cities, and habitat destruction.[11] In order to keep our crops and wildlife habitats in working order, we need to support scientists who study insect population trends. We also need to protect the insects' future, our food supply, and the continued life of the planet's flowers and meadows.

Have you thought about the fact that God designed the pollinators to grow the flowers and to "clothe" the grass of the field?

A Biblical Perspective

We can learn a lot about what God is like by looking at nature. In Luke 12:27–28, Jesus said, "Consider how the wild flowers grow. They do not labor or spin. . . . That is how God clothes the grass of the field" (NIV).

God uses creativity to make everyday things happen! He assigned the insects to pollinate the flowers we love and to help

grow the crops we eat. When it comes to giving us the things we need, God is a practical problem-solver and worthy of our trust.

A Lesson from Insects

The insects have something to teach us. Isaiah 40:22 says God "sits above the circle of the earth, and its inhabitants are like grasshoppers." Just as we're compared to flowers in Luke, here we're compared to grasshoppers—we're here for a short time and then gone, and our bodies return to the dust. Like grasshoppers, our lives are short and busy, hopping from thing to thing, but God isn't limited by a short lifespan. The God who spoke the world into being is the same one who listens to our prayers right now!

Whether we have half an hour to clean our room, two minutes to brush our teeth, or seventy-plus years to live for God, it's easier to accomplish a task when we stay focused because we know how much time it takes. The Bible tells us that being aware of how short our lives can be teaches us "to number our days, that we may gain a heart of wisdom" (Psalm 90:12 NIV).

What would change in your life if you lived out your faith like a grasshopper?

This truth should remind each of us to live our lives connected to God.

He has plans that will outlast our lives, but He invites us to take part in them anyway. How cool is that! For whatever length of time we're here on this earth, we can be intentional and focused on doing God's work. Ephesians 2:10 tells us, "For we are God's handiwork, created in Christ Jesus to do good works, which God prepared in advance for us to do" (NIV). This good work includes our environmental care and actions.

The Resilience of Insects

Earth's bugs disappear by the billions. They're consumed by other animals, killed by changes in the weather, and easily stepped on without notice. You might think they would have been wiped out a long time ago. But bugs are great at bouncing back. When connected to their community, they can multiply at an amazing rate. Even though their lifespans can be as short as a few days, their happy noises and endless activity aren't affected by the problems they face.

How can you choose the right attitude when bad things happen to you? How does that attitude help you care for creation?

Can you think of some other species that faces trouble, but bounces back when connected to a strong community? One that praises God with happy noises and endless activity no matter what?

That's right, God's people are called to be like bugs! Paul explained what it was like for the apostles to live this way. "When reviled, we bless; when persecuted, we endure; when slandered, we entreat. We have become, and are still, like the scum of the world, the refuse of all things" (1 Corinthians 4:12–13). What Paul is saying is this: when we get stepped on, threatened, cursed, and snuffed out, Christians can choose to bounce back and multiply, welcoming even more people into God's family because of what we went through.

How we react to the bad things that happen is a choice. It is the choice Christians are supposed to make so the world can see what God's love does in our lives. When it comes to the problems our planet is facing, our reaction should be the same. Instead of rolling over and accepting the bad things that happen, Christians should choose to help things bounce back! After all, one of the first responsibilities God gave people was to take care of creation, and that responsibility hasn't stopped.

HOW YOU CAN MAKE A DIFFERENCE

PRACTICE POLLINATOR-FRIENDLY LAWN CARE

Some lawn care methods inadvertently harm or kill pollinators. Help stop harmful practices in your lawn and protect pollinator health.

Create a pollinator-friendly mowing schedule

- Ask your caregivers to mow the yard once every two weeks. This has proven the best for bee populations, with 30 percent more bees visiting lawns mowed every other week.[12]
- The every-two-weeks mowing schedule provides local bees with foraging habitat through the growth of clover and dandelion. Let the clovers and dandelions bloom for a bit!

Add wilderness charm

🔹 Add some native wildflowers to your yard. They will attract and support beautiful butterflies, bees, and birds.

🔹 Grow edible plants that will attract pollinators. Here are some to consider: squash, basil, green beans, lavender, apple trees, radishes, and sunflowers.

Leave debris

🔹 Piles of branches, dead leaves, and old trees make ideal homes for insects. Even small, hidden piles are a kindness!

PLANT A POLLINATOR GARDEN

You can help save pollinators by making your yard more hospitable to them with a pollinator garden. If you do this with your church or neighborhood, it's a wonderful way to serve your community.

Pollinator garden tips

🔹 Pollinator gardens require native plants for the best results. Your region will have specific conditions for specific plants.

🔹 The Xerces Society has a database of native pollinator plants for each region. You can also look up native plants on Audubon's database with your zip code.

- Choose a variety of plants that bloom from early spring into late fall. Include night-blooming flowers for bats and moths.
- It's a good idea to plant perennials—plants that grow back each year without needing to be replanted—because they need less maintenance.
- Designate a space with full or partial sunlight and use that nutrient-rich compost you made (remember from chapter six?) when you turn over the soil.

BUILD A MONARCH WAYSTATION

Monarchs migrate long distances and need stopover points, as well as habitats for feeding and laying eggs. Milkweed habitats are a game changer for monarchs to make a comeback. Make a waystation at your home, school, or church.

Plant native milkweed

- Monarch caterpillars are specialists, which means they eat *only* one kind of plant to turn into butterflies: milkweed. Talk about picky eaters! If you want to help the monarch caterpillars turn into butterflies, you could plant your local native varieties of milkweed. Be sure to plant at least two types.

Plant native nectar flowers

- Monarchs require nectar from flowers for daily food, but especially for the energy needed to migrate from North America to overwintering grounds in Mexico.
- Start a new garden or add various nectar flowers to your current garden.

Strategically set up your butterfly stopping spot

- Milkweed and nectar plants grow best in sunny areas in lighter soils (or with low clay content). Find an area where they will receive at least six hours of sun each day.
- Avoid places where water pools in your yard. This will prevent root rot and allow for the soil to breathe.[13]

Certify your monarch waystation

- Certify your monarch habitat through Monarch Watch online and receive a nifty sign to hang, plus a spot on the interactive map of other waystation neighbors.

BUILD OR BUY A BAT BOX

Provide for and support bats in your yard, and they will thank you by eating thousands of mosquitoes while also pollinating at night. Plus guano, or bat droppings, is an excellent natural fertilizer for gardens.

Bat box tips

- You can provide a home for bats by building a bat box. Bat Conservation International's website provides free downloadable instructions for two kinds: four-chamber and rocket boxes. They also have a map that shows what colors to paint your box depending on your region.
- Bat boxes can be purchased online by grown-ups as well. If they buy a few, you could get friends together for a crafting party and decorate them with your own personal touch.
- If bats are in your home, contact your local natural resource agency to have them humanely removed.

LIMIT OR STOP USING SYNTHETIC
PESTICIDES AND HERBICIDES

Pesticides kill bugs, and herbicides kill weeds. That's why they are popular. But that's also what makes them dangerous to the environment. Pesticides are toxic to the environment (and some are known to cause cancer in humans). Look up Beyond Pesticides for specific guidance on how to control particular pests or weeds using alternatives to pesticides.

Creative alternatives

- Nontoxic alternatives to pesticides include neem oil and diatomaceous earth (use carefully and sparingly because they can also kill beneficial insects).
- Natural predators like ladybugs (really, ladybugs are fierce!) for plants and nematodes for the soil (which feed on more than two hundred pests) are also helpful.[14] Plant insectary plants (ones that attract helpful bugs) such as mint, rosemary, thyme, and marigold.
- To get rid of unwanted bugs, attract other insect-eating wildlife like birds by building a nesting box and adding bird feeders.
- Mulching is an eco-friendly way of preventing weeds, but check to make sure the mulch doesn't include herbicides.

SUPPORT AND VOLUNTEER WITH
CONSERVATION ORGANIZATIONS

Check out nonprofits that help pollinators

- Check out The Nature Conservancy, Bat Conservation International, and Xerces for ways to support pollinators.

Get involved in a citizen science project

Become a citizen scientist! You can help count and monitor insect populations in your area and report your data to a project in the works. Grab a grown-up and check out Xerces to get started.

CHAPTER EIGHT

WETLANDS
Nature's Beautiful Borders

For this water goes there, that the waters of the sea may become fresh; so everything will live where the river goes.

EZEKIEL 47:9

What do you call the wet lands found between different kinds of habitats? Wetlands! Okay, so whoever named wetlands wasn't super creative. In fact, the name can be kind of confusing because not all wetlands are wet all the time. So what are wetlands, and why do they matter?

Wetlands are the areas that border and protect other ecosystems. They're the "transition zones" between

land and water worlds. They do important jobs for every habitat they touch.

Wetlands naturally filter and store harmful toxins and keep them from reaching our water systems and contaminating our water supply. They are also nature's way of preventing storm damage and soaking up water during floods. The roots of their plants strengthen the soil structure of the earth to fight against erosion. Did you have any idea that wetlands were so uniquely significant?

Many species rely on wetlands. Fish and shellfish use them for their nurseries—the habitat for their eggs—and for shelter and food. Migratory birds—birds that fly south for the winter because winters are cold!—count on them for stopover points during their long journeys. In the continental US, wetlands take up only about 5 percent of the land area, but nearly half of all North American birds feed or nest in wetlands, while one-third of our endangered and threatened species depend on them.[1]

Wetlands also help prevent *harmful algal blooms* (HAB). HABs happen when bodies of water are overloaded with nutrients. Sounds like a good thing, right? Nutrients are what living creatures need to survive. But algae are greedy beasties that eat up the nutrients, sucking out a lot of the oxygen in the water. This leads to massive fish kills since fish need oxygen too, even if they get it through gills and not their mouths like we do. Some algal blooms are toxic to humans, known as *red tides* for the crimson color you can see from the shore and even from space. Wetlands

Most algae aren't bad, though! In fact, scientists are working on ways to use algae to convert sunlight into useable fuel.

WHAT ARE WETLANDS?

Wetlands are an area of land flooded or saturated with water seasonally or year-round. So they might be covered with water only when rivers or streams overflow, but they might also be covered with water all the time. They feature plants that love living in watery conditions. The water can be salty, fresh, or somewhere in between, depending on where the wetland is located. Wetlands by the coast are mostly salty and surround **estuaries**, which are partially enclosed bodies of water where rivers run into the sea, creating brackish (mix of fresh and salty) waters. Inland wetlands are usually fresh and located by lakes, ponds, and streams. They also pop up in prairies and can spring up in areas where groundwater rises to the surface.

work to absorb excess nutrients from fertilizer runoff and help prevent harmful algal blooms in rivers, lakes, and estuaries.

There are three main types of wetlands: swamps, marshes, and bogs.

Swamps are like flooded forests with fluctuating water levels. Cypress, willow, and mangrove are common swamp trees. In the coastal tropics, mangroves' impressive root systems provide cage-like shelter for crabs, conchs, shrimp, and even seals.

Marshes are dominated by grasses and shrubs and are loved by many birds, like the red-winged blackbird, great egret, and swarms of swallows, which find plenty of crabs and insects to feed on within the mud and vegetation.

Bogs are found farther north in colder climates such as Canada, Russia, and even the Arctic. They look like lakes filled with the collected debris of leaves, roots, and stems with moss and heather growing over the surface. Bogs are often home to gnarly carnivorous plants, like the pitcher plant and horned bladderwort, which lure, trap, and digest small invertebrates, but bogs also grow pleasant things like cranberries.

The Importance of Wetlands

Wetlands are the most underrated ecosystems on our planet, and they're vanishing three times faster than forests.[2] They're the habitat connectors, benefiting and supporting each ecosystem they touch. We've come a long way in understanding their importance and in taking steps to protect and restore them, but more needs to be done.

Mangroves provide homes for thousands of species, prevent erosion, filter pollution, and protect the land from waves and storms. They filter up to 90 percent of salt from seawater. The destruction of mangroves in wetlands leads to coastal damage and increased flooding, along with the release of large amounts of carbon dioxide into the atmosphere.

The Mangrove Ecosystem

BACTERIA

WHITE
IBIS

GREAT BLUE
HERON

ALLIGATOR

BARNACLES

MANGROVE CRAB

GRASS
SHRIMP

ORANGE
SPONGE

COMMON
SNOOK FISH

PINFISH

HERMIT
CRAB

CUSHION SEA STAR

The Disappearance of Wetlands

We've lost more than half of our wetlands. They used to be seen as useless. We filled them in to create farmlands, and we drained them and built cities—including San Francisco, Lansing, St. Louis, and Washington, DC. As our population grows and more people move to cities, wetlands are being converted to either living spaces or places to grow food. Today, wetlands are threatened by water drainage, pollution, invasive species, mismanaged dams, upstream erosion, and sediment dumping from deforestation.[3]

The coasts of the lower forty-eight US states lose eighty thousand acres of wetlands yearly.[4] This is around seven football fields of wetlands lost every hour! One main reason for wetland loss on the coasts is development, since nearly half of the US population lives on the coasts. This loss threatens sustainable fisheries, endangered species, clean water supply, and shoreline protection from storms, floods, and tides. When we lose wetlands, coastal communities are more at risk to damage from strong storms, like Hurricane Katrina in 2005, the most expensive natural disaster in US history to date.

Restoring and Building Wetlands

Remember India's complex water problems from chapter one— flooding during monsoons and wells running dry in droughts? Restoring and building wetlands is one thing communities can do to avoid those problems. Laying down concrete and other hard surfaces in development projects blocks rainwater from reaching the ground and makes floods worse. Wetlands, on the other hand,

> Did you know that wetlands are one of the most productive ecosystems? Forty percent of all the species we've discovered on our planet use wetlands as a place to live or breed.[5]

soak up water and help to refill the groundwater in aquifers, storing up extra water for dry periods.

As we've come to realize the small but powerful ways wetlands protect and provide for the rest of the planet and for us, we've put protections in place and begun restoring many areas. Ramsar is an international convention to safeguard the world's wetland habitats. It provides a framework for countries to wisely manage wetlands and their resources, but getting people to follow the rules is often challenging.

It's super important that we continue to protect and restore our wetlands. What's at stake? More intense flooding, storm damage, dangerous algal blooms, diminishing fish stocks, and toxins contaminating water sources! Wetlands also add a touch of nature's beauty and serenity amid busy urban and suburban lives, providing us with recreational activities like kayaking, fishing, and bird watching. They should be a prized part of our cities, neighborhoods, and public lands. They're a nature-based solution to a lot of different environmental problems around the world, from water scarcity to pollution to endangered species.

Our Responsibility

There's a lot we can do to help restore natural areas like the wetlands. We just need to find the right mix of technological and natural solutions. For example, when people build houses near the beach, they could build a concrete seawall—a big wall meant to stop the water from flooding their house—or they could leave some wetlands between their house and the water since wetlands naturally lessen storm damage and help prevent floods. When we work with nature's abilities to guard our coasts, we're developing what's known as "living shorelines," a growing nature-based strategy around our waterways.

We need to make sure that our hopes for saving the planet don't just rely on what we can do and what we can build (but those things definitely help). The desire to save the world comes from the heart of God, and He wants to partner with us in our efforts to fix what's broken. God has given us an example of how to see wisdom in the wetlands. When we look at nature as God made it, we'll find other ways to restore the planet too!

> People used to think the wetlands weren't very important. What is something that became important to you once you understood it better?

A Biblical Perspective

What does Scripture have to say about taking care of our wetlands? Like a lot of the choices we make every day, including environmental choices, the Bible points us to the value of wisdom in handling complicated issues. There's not just one thing we can do that will fix the environment for everyone everywhere (wouldn't it be nice if there was?!). How we take care of the land requires us to use our best judgment every time. What may work in one area may not in another. But we can and should do something.

God's Wise Design

Wetlands probably aren't the first topic you think of for earth care, but in His wisdom, God often appoints things the world overlooks as insignificant and small—think fishermen disciples or children—for His grand design. God created the wetlands ecosystems to soak up the toxins and salt and to produce life and keep it going. What a great surprise! As Christians, we shouldn't be surprised that God uses the places that seem useless, because as you may have noticed, God is always working wonders through His creation and through the things we go through. God shows us the kind of God He is by using the unexpected places to work out His plan. And guess what! That's exactly how these often-unnoticed places work! The wetlands—swamps and **fens** and reedy river overflows—are literally protecting and providing for you and me, even when we don't notice it.

Nature's Wisdom in Harmony

As we look for wisdom to solve the challenges of caring for our planet, we should work toward solutions that bring peace and connection where everyone can win. This kind of wisdom looks at different options from different angles and finds solutions that help each part or person involved.

How does this work? Let's look at an example.

Can you think of any problems or challenges you've faced that had more than one solution? How did you come up with the answer that worked best?

Cities grow when people move in, usually because there are more jobs to be found in cities than in the country. To make room for the people who want to move in, developers—people who plan out where buildings get built—change the land into something that can be useful for homes and businesses. That sometimes means that forests, fields, farmlands, and fens (which is a kind of wetland) get paved over and turned into skyscrapers.

But the people who live in cities need more than homes and jobs. They also need clean air and water and land that doesn't flood whenever it rains. Wise planning means looking at all the needs—homes, jobs, clean air, a lack of flooding—and rethinking how to develop a city in ways that can help everyone win.

Vancouver, Canada, did just that. They built and grew a wetland in the middle of the city near a stream (where it's home to the city's beaver resident, Justin Beaver!). Wetlands are a nature-based, long-lasting solution to many environmental problems for our cities, coasts, grasslands, and forests.

We often turn to technology and human inventions to solve our problems, which isn't a bad thing. But as Christians, we should also look at how God designed nature to be a wise guide for caring for His world. Often, nature's solutions don't sound very impressive, but when we take time to understand how God designed things to work (like the functioning of wetlands), we can use His ingenuity to solve our problems in natural ways.

HOW YOU CAN MAKE A DIFFERENCE

GET TO KNOW THE WETLANDS IN YOUR AREA

Wetlands are surprisingly easy to find! They're on the coasts, in parks, and even in the area between divided highways and low-lying areas in cities, towns, and forests. You may be near some of the bigger US landmarks with wetlands like the Great Lakes, Gulf of Mexico, Long Island Sound, Chesapeake Bay, or San Francisco Bay.

Explore your local wetlands

- Look into your local parks or contact your parks and recreation department to find out where the wetlands are near you. Put on some boots and long-sleeved shirts—mosquitoes love the wetlands too—and go check them out!
- Find a field guide and learn even more about the wonders of wetland habitats, like how they benefit the systems around them through the animals and plants that live there.
- Wetlands have exclusive plant types suited to the specific conditions of wetness and salt levels. Find out which ones grow in the wetlands near you and see how many you can find!

Advocate for wetland protections in your area

- Write a letter to your city, county, state, or national lawmakers and let them know how important wetlands are to you and to the earth. Maybe even draw them a picture of a wetland in your town or state to go with it.

BRING THE WETLANDS TO YOU

Our lawns are part of the larger watersheds of our area, which drain into nearby streams and wetlands when it rains. Rain gardens in yards slow the water flow and allow the ground and plants to absorb and naturally treat the water before it reaches streams and wetlands.

Plant a rain garden

- When it rains, water collects and flows from your roof, driveway, and other hard surfaces. A rain garden catches the runoff, allowing it to soak into the ground and filter out pollutants.

- A rain garden is a garden of native shrubs, perennials, and flowers planted in the lowest area of your yard (where the rainwater tends to pool).

- Plant native vegetation (plants that normally grow where you live) in your rain garden. Some native plants like lots of sun and water. Some don't. Be sure to consider that when picking what to plant.

DESIGN YOUR OWN CITY

Just like Vancouver, Canada, you can design a city that uses nature as part of the landscape. Let your imagination run wild. What will your city be called? What kind of climate does it have? Does it get a lot of rainfall or little? Is there a river running through it or is it on the ocean or is it in the middle of the desert? You decide!

Figure out the shape of your city

- Grab a blank piece of paper and a few coins. It'll work best if you have different kinds of coins to work with—pennies, nickels, dimes, and quarters. Toss the coins onto the blank paper. If one rolls off, just toss it back on. Then draw a line to circle in all the coins. This is the shape of your city.

Draw some landmarks

- You get to decide what the different kinds of coins mean. If you connect two pennies that are on opposite sides of your city, you could have a river or a highway. Maybe the nickels are for a mountain range or a desert. Draw a few different kinds of ecosystems if you want to!
- Be sure to add some wetlands between the different kinds of ecosystems in your city. Think about what might be the best place for a wetland (like near a building or homes that will have runoff with toxins and fertilizer).

Tell your city's story

- With your map in front of you, write up what things are happening in the city. Are there any endangered species who depend on your wetlands? Is someone trying to help them succeed? Use the landmarks—the river, roads, and mountains—as you write. Work them into the story. Be sure to give everyone a happy ending!

SUPPORT NONPROFITS WORKING TO PROTECT AND RESTORE WETLANDS

- Ducks Unlimited focuses on wetland protection and restoration across the US and Canada.
- Visit the Environmental Protection Agency (EPA) website for examples of state and local wetland monitoring programs. Go to epa.gov/wetlands for resources and contacts. Also look into EPA regional contacts, US Army Corps of Engineers (USACE) contacts, and Association of State Wetland Managers to get involved in wetland projects near you.

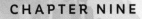

CHAPTER NINE

CORAL REEFS
Earth's Underwater Playground

In his teaching the islands will put their hope.

ISAIAH 42:4 (NIV)

Have you seen the movie *Finding Nemo*? When Nemo the clown fish is taken from his anemone home in the Great Barrier Reef off the coast of Australia, his dad, Marlin, journeys across the ocean to find and rescue his son. The movie features clown fish, angelfish, rays, seahorses, starfish, and more. It's a fun movie and a great introduction to life beneath the waves. But the sad truth is that our coral reefs are in as much danger as Nemo is of not getting home.

Although coral reefs take

up less than 1 percent of the planet's oceans, nearly 25 percent of all marine creatures rely on them.[1] Their biodiversity is so great, they're dubbed the "rainforest of the sea." Yet largely due to human actions, they're in grave trouble. If we don't make changes now, within this century we could lose our coral reefs![2]

The Destruction of Coral

While some of the coral reef destruction is due to natural occurrences, unfortunately a lot of the major damage has been caused by humans. Oftentimes we aren't thinking about the accidental consequences of our choices, like if your new sweater shrinks to toy-size in the dryer. By becoming educated and more aware of the impact of our human actions, we can stop the damage being done to coral reefs, a spectacular part of God's creation.

WHAT IS CORAL?

Corals are animals. Their soft bodies have fat, little bases with tentacles called polyps extending up into the water. They may look like plants attached to rocks and hard surfaces, but the coral polyps move, growing and shrinking in the water. These animals construct the giant sea architecture of the reefs. They do this by building layer upon layer of the limestone reefs, which become habitat for fish, urchins, sponges, sharks, rays, lobsters, octopuses, snails, and more.

Warming Waters

From 2014 to 2017, unu-sually warm waters hit 70 percent of coral reefs around the world in a massive coral bleaching event.[3] Australia's Great Barrier Reef—where *Finding Nemo* was set—saw hundreds of miles of corals turn from vibrant colors to chalky white. About half of

Australia's Great Barrier Reef died followed the warming events of 2016 and 2017, and it may never fully recover.[4]

Coral bleaching happens when the corals are stressed by changes in external conditions, like warming waters, and react by shooting out the algae that live inside them. The algae provide the corals with their food and their color, so when they eject them, the corals turn white and become deathly ill. Humans play a major part in the warmer waters due to the greenhouse gases we put into the atmosphere.[5] While corals can recover from bleaching, they need cooler water and steady conditions to get better, which can take a really long time.

Overfishing, Pollution, and Buildup

In addition to warming ocean waters, other threats to coral reefs are making things harder. Overfishing and other destructive human practices around the reefs lessen our fish supply, which can really mess with the reefs. In a healthy coral reef ecosystem,

Anatomy of a Reef

MOUTH

POLYPS

TENTACLES

GUT
CAVITY

TISSUE
CONNECTION
BETWEEN POLYPS

MESENTERIAL
FILAMENTS

BARE SKELETON
OF POLYP

fish feed on the algae. Without them, the algae build up too much around the coral, ultimately suffocating them and blocking the sunlight, leading to the reef dying off.

The pollution we contribute from things like plastic, sewage, and oil is also poisoning reefs. And when dirt from human construction, logging, and mining reaches the ocean from beaches and rivers, the reefs become smothered by sediment buildup.

Pollution, sediments, toxins, chemicals, and excessive nutrients reach the coasts by traveling downstream, eventually flowing into the ocean. This messes with coastal habitats, including tide pools, and it's especially bad for coral reefs. With coral bleaching and the other dangers they face, corals need pollution-free water if they're going to have a chance at survival.

Human activity is also causing our oceans to become more acidic at a scary rate. Think about it for a minute. Would you want to take a bath in clean water or unusually acidic water? Simple, daily activities like driving cars or using electricity put carbon dioxide into the air, which is then absorbed into the ocean, making it slightly more acidic. This makes it challenging for corals to build their reefs, and if the water reaches a certain level of acidity, the reefs can literally begin to dissolve.

The coral reef is made of thousands of polyps. This illustration shows the basic anatomy of a single polyp—the main part affected by coral bleaching. Bleaching happens when corals get rid of the algae that live inside their tissue, causing them to fade, often turning completely white.

Tide pools are amazing! They are shallow pools filled with all kinds of life—starfish, barnacles, anemones, periwinkle snails, small fish, and more—that connect to the ocean at high tide and are their own little habitat during low tide. If you see a tide pool, feel free to bring a bag with you and pick up any plastic, metal, or trash that doesn't belong, but leave the animals and plants in place!

The Importance of Coral

Corals are more than admirable architects of the ocean; we'd be in serious trouble if we lost them. They protect coasts from storm damage and support the local economy. We also count on reefs as a food source, and we've discovered how to make some kinds of medicines from their ecosystems. More than half a billion people rely on coral reefs for food, money, and protection. If putting a price on it helps you understand the benefits of coral reefs, the value of the world's coral reefs is estimated to be nearly tens of billions of US dollars per year.[6] But even if they weren't worth a dime, God still made them and we should recognize them as our oceans' natural treasures.

A Biblical Perspective

God built His creation to work so when everything is in balance, the results can be absolutely dazzling. You see, the coral reefs are made up of multiple species living closely together in harmony. The algae and coral need each other for nutrition and protection— they struggle to survive without one another.

Symbiotic Ecosystem

This **symbiotic relationship** between algae and coral helps bring about the bright colors corals are known for. God saw that *it was good* to meet the practical needs of coral reefs in a way that makes them beautiful. He provides for His creation and gives it beauty all at once.

How can this underwater symbiotic design teach us to interact with nature? Well, given that about 40 percent of the world's population lives near our coasts, we need to champion the perfect teamwork that God

Symbiotic relationships exist when two different things work together in ways that help them both. They are the peanut butter and jelly of the natural world. Actually, they are more like sea anemones and hermit crabs.

Sea anemones like to stick to hermit crab shells and eat the leftovers of whatever the crabs catch to eat. Hermit crabs enjoy having the sea anemones on their backs because the anemones fight off predators that would eat the crabs. Teamwork makes the dream work!

designed for these ecosystems. We work, play, learn, fish, eat, and live our lives right by these amazing coastal habitats and share the space daily. We must acknowledge that we are *in relationship* with these reefs, and we have been blessed with a chance to keep them beautiful. Coral reefs are God's underwater gardens and a legacy of His creative work, which we're called to look after.

Trusting God

As caretakers of nature, we should be careful not to take too much from it. But people do take too much. Why? Because when someone finds a good thing (fish, money that comes from selling fish, money in general), they might think that more of that thing will make them happy or secure. The problem, especially with overfishing, is that taking too much out of the ocean now will mean we can't get anything out of the ocean later.

Greedy actions are often motivated by the fear that we will not have enough or be provided for. But as we can see from God's design in nature, He will provide for us. That's who He is. He is a provider.

Look at the reefs. The corals absorb tiny algae with their tentacles, the seahorses find homes in the crannies and nooks of the reefs, and the clown fish find refuge in the anemones (Remember Nemo and Marlin?). Every unique creature is considered and provided for through the way God designed coral reefs to work. And

By overfishing—taking out too many of one kind of fish so people can eat it—we make it harder for the bigger fish that would normally eat those fish to have enough food. Plus, when the fish run out, we no longer can fish them for food either!

guess what? The result is *beautiful*! How much more will God take care of us and give us the good things we need (Matthew 7:11)? We can rest knowing that God provides for His creation, and this comfort can stir us to be generous toward nature, particularly the reefs.

HOW YOU CAN MAKE A DIFFERENCE

MINDFULLY VISIT TOURIST SPOTS AS A GRACIOUS, GREEN GUEST

Keep these recreation and tourism tips in mind

Every year, families from all over the country head to the coasts to enjoy the wind, waves, surf, and sun. This kind of tourism supports more than 6.5 million jobs.[7] Unfortunately, coastal tourism and development can also be a source of harm to coastal environments like coral reefs. If your family is heading to the beach this summer, be a caring, careful traveler and leave the area better than you found it.

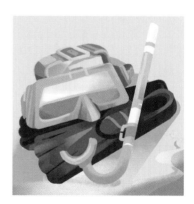

Recreation and tourism tips

- If you dive or snorkel, don't touch or disrupt corals. Stirring up sediment can smother them. Enjoy with your eyes only, not your hands.
- Don't buy coral products or shark teeth or sand dollars as

souvenirs. Find a cool shark figurine, snazzy airbrushed T-shirt, or literally anything else not taken from the sea.

- If your family rents a boat, avoid dropping your boat anchor or chain near a coral reef; look for a sandy bottom or use available moorings.
- Chemicals in sunscreen can build up in coral tissues and cause bleaching, damage, deformation, and even death. Protect your skin and protect coral—buy only marine-friendly sunscreen. Check out the National Oceanic and Atmospheric Administration's (NOAA) sunscreen webpage for more information.

BE RESPONSIBLE FOR THE REEFS, NO MATTER YOUR LOCATION

Keep your yards watershed friendly

- No matter where you live, the things that happen in your yard can end up in bodies of water and habitats downstream.
- Pick up litter in a neighborhood or city area with a church group; especially target trash near stormwater drains.

Volunteer at beach cleanups

- Planning a family trip to the beach this summer? Set aside some time to get involved in beach or reef cleanups while you're there. Don't have beach travel plans yet? Now you've got a good reason to make some!
- Visit the websites for the Ocean Conservancy, Surfrider Foundation, Ocean Blue Project, or a local coastal organization to learn about opportunities to help.

CHOOSE SUSTAINABLE SEAFOOD

Did you know that, as of 2020, 3.3 billion people around the world rely on fish as a main protein source in their diet? And that number is only growing. Unfortunately, the number of sustainable fisheries has not been keeping up with global demands.

Compare these numbers taken from the Food and Agriculture Organization of the United Nations (FAO): In 1990, 90 percent of fish stocks were within biologically sustainable levels. In 2017, it was only 65.8 percent.[8]

Whether you love tuna sandwiches, fish sticks, or Goldfish crackers (just kidding, those are only shaped like fish), try to make sure the seafood you eat comes from a fishery that's not crashing fish populations. Fish are an important part of the coastal food web, and they also help keep algae in check that could otherwise outcompete and smother coral.

Make informed seafood purchases to help prevent overfishing

- We don't have to give up seafood altogether, but it helps to make sure our seafood is sustainably sourced to prevent overfishing.
- Look for certification labels from the Marine Stewardship Council (MSC), Aquaculture Stewardship Council (ASC), Global Seafood Alliance, Best Aquaculture Practices (BAP), Friend of the Sea, and Naturland.

Favor locally caught seafood

- Join a community-supported fishery (CSF) and help support local fishermen and promote sustainable practices. Visit localcatch.org to find a CSF near you.

- If a CSF isn't an option for you, ask questions and be choosy about your seafood purchases. If you don't know where the fish come from, you can always write a letter and ask. Businesses love getting letters from kids like you!

CHECK OUT THESE NONPROFITS

These nonprofits are working to save coral reefs:

- Mission Blue works to set up marine protected areas (MPA) that protect coral reefs and other valuable marine life from fishing and other potentially harmful human activities.
- The Coral Reef Alliance's mission is to save coral reefs around the world. It works with coastal communities to lessen threats to reefs, like dealing with sewage and waste management issues, and it researches how reefs adapt to climate change to come up with new solutions.
- The Nature Conservancy is an organization on the forefront of living shoreline development to help coastal communities prepare for sea level rise and intense storms, among many other things. There may also be local environmental organizations in your area working to promote living shoreline solutions, like Save the Sound in Connecticut and New York.

CHAPTER TEN

THE OCEAN

Our Large and Mysterious Waters

Who spread out the earth upon the waters, His love endures forever.

PSALM 136:6 (NIV)

When you think about the ocean, what do you picture? Maybe you think about beach balls, sandcastles, and seagulls snatching ice cream cones from unsuspecting people (it happens!). Or maybe you picture whales swimming in the deep, dolphins jumping out of the water, or sharks planning their next meal. Our oceans are beautiful, mysterious, and large, and yet they're suffering because of human activity and careless choices.

WHAT IS THE OCEAN?

The ocean is one connected, colossal body of saltwater covering more than 70 percent of the surface of planet Earth. We divide it up geographically into four or five regions: the Pacific, Atlantic, Indian, Southern (there's still debate about this one in the scientific community), and Arctic oceans. Around 97 percent of the world's water fills the ocean basins. This volume moves and churns within and between each region through currents (which are like rivers in the ocean) and gyres (which are large, spinning currents). These massive forces mix the ocean and influence its biology down to the tiniest marine critters, the plankton.

The oceans are home to abundant sea life. They've been used to transport people since Noah built the ark. They are important for businesses and seafood eaters. And oceans help regulate the climate too! But while humans enjoy the oceans for lots of different reasons, we've also used them as watery garbage dumps. The litter that finds its way to the seas forms slowly spinning whirlpools of trash called *garbage patches*. The pollution we've made is disrupting and destroying life at every level.

The Problems Affecting Our Oceans

We have several challenges facing us as we look at the problems facing our oceans. Although the problems are definitely big, they can be solved when we do our part as individuals. Then, when others see what we're doing, they might be inspired to join us.

Pollution

Pollution in our oceans is a huge problem. After production, 79 percent of plastic is "thrown away" in the trash (often after only one use) and taken to a landfill,[1] or "thrown away" into nature. Without change and action, by 2050 there will be more pounds of plastic in the ocean than pounds of fish.[2] That's shocking!

Let's look at it another way. Blue whales are the largest animals on the planet. They can be around one hundred feet in length (or about three school buses in a row) and weigh up to two hundred tons. Big, right? Now, picture eighty million blue whales. That's roughly the weight of plastic that enters our ocean every year.[3] With all that plastic ending up in the ocean, there's no wonder we have garbage patches swirling around, turning bits of the ocean into a "trash soup" of tiny plastic bits polluting the water.

The largest example of trash accumulating in the ocean is the Great Pacific Garbage Patch, which floats between Hawaii and California. If you are picturing a solid island made up of plastic bags and forgotten toys, think again. Plastic in the ocean gets smaller over time, but it

Blue whales are huge! Their tongues can weigh as much as an elephant, and their hearts as much as a car. But as big as they are, they eat teeny-tiny animals called krill—sometimes as much as four tons of the little shrimplike animals in a day. Unfortunately, blue whales are currently on the endangered animals list, and all the plastic in the ocean isn't going to help them out.

never completely breaks down. The Great Pacific Garbage Patch is mostly made up of microscopic bits of plastic mixed with larger items (old fishing nets, shoes, and rubber ducks), but it looks more like cloudy trash soup than an island.

While the Great Pacific Garbage Patch is the most famous garbage patch, there's trash floating around all five of the ocean's swirling gyres. Plastic trash that washes into rivers, lakes, and oceans is hurting watery environments in a lot of different ways.

Microplastics

The majority of the plastic pieces, called *microplastics*, have been broken down and are very small. Microplastics are a major issue because fish, sea birds, and other sea creatures eat them. For example, albatrosses are giant seabirds that look like a mix between a seagull and pelican. They skim the ocean surface with their beaks to scoop up food, but instead they often pick up plastic. On Midway Atoll, a group of Hawaiian Islands, decaying albatrosses were found with abdomens full of shards of plastic and bottle caps.

It's a sad shock—their stomachs become trash bags for our litter.

Plastic has been discovered in 59 percent of seabirds,[4] in all sea turtle species,[5] and in more than 25 percent of the fish in world sea markets.[6] The smaller particles are also known to soak up toxins from the environment. That means when they get eaten by sea creatures, the toxins can build up in their systems and affect everything in the food chain above them, all the way up to humans, a process called **bioaccumulation**. We don't know all the ways that plastic litter is coming back to haunt us, but we do know enough to be concerned about it.

Ocean Acidification (Carbon Pollution)

Another type of pollution that's negatively affecting our oceans is carbon pollution. A problem called *ocean acidification* occurs when there is too much carbon dioxide (from vehicles and factories) in the atmosphere that is then naturally absorbed by the ocean waters. Oceans absorb around 30 percent of the CO_2 released into the air.[7] This increases the acidity of the water and affects the wildlife of the sea. Many marine species are used to surviving at specific acidity levels, and when those levels go up and down, things get dangerous for those species.

This is especially true for sea creatures that rely on calcium

Plankton is more of a classification than a specific animal. The name describes the tiny—often single-celled—organisms that make up the bottom rung of the ocean's food chain. Plantlike plankton organisms are called phytoplankton. Animal-like plankton organisms are called zooplankton.

carbonate for their shells and homes, because calcium carbonate dissolves under more acidic conditions. We've already discussed one animal this impacts—corals. Ocean acidification is also bad news for the shellfish we use as a productive food source—things like shrimp, crayfish, crabs, lobsters, oysters, and clams. Finally, certain types of plankton—tiny free-floating organisms that make up the base of the ocean's food web—are especially fragile to the high-carbon waters. This can in turn impact populations of fish that eat them and then the bigger sea creatures, like dolphins and seals, that count on these fish for food.

Overfishing

Another challenge for our oceans is overfishing. Fish stocks crash when we take away too many and don't let the fish populations build back up. The exact number is often debated by conservation scientists, but the UN estimates that about a third of global fisheries are overharvested.[8] This practice threatens not only the fisheries and people who depend on them to make a living, it also threatens our food security and the protein supply billions of people depend on around the world. Fishing itself isn't wrong, but it's unwise and shortsighted to

Blue crabs—one of the most eaten shellfish varieties around the world—help manage populations of the animals and fish they eat (and they'll eat just about anything). To grow, these crabs shed their shells and hide out until their new, larger shells grow hard. As the ocean grows more acidic, blue crabs will have a much harder time growing shells at all.

deplete the resource rapidly. We're stealing from our futures. In certain areas, like the US coasts, there have recently been encouraging signs that some fisheries are on the path to recovery thanks to sustainable fishing enforcement, but we still have a lot of work to do.

The Importance of the Ocean

It's difficult to overstate how important oceans are to the health of our entire planet. The oceans help to regulate the climate by moving heat from the equator to the poles. We count on oceans for around half of the oxygen produced on earth;[9] most of this comes from tiny **photosynthesizing** plankton (they're amazing!). Kelp forests and seagrass beds capture carbon dioxide (in a good way that doesn't hurt coral or shellfish) and are an important part of climate change solutions. The ocean affects other necessities like our weather, breathing, and food. Plus, it's an unending source of exploration, recreation, and wonder.

Setting up what are called marine protected areas (MPA) is a key method of restoring the oceans. These areas establish rules to create no-fishing zones that help protect ocean habitats (like coral reefs and kelp forests) and allow areas to bounce back. Billions of people rely on fish from the ocean for their main source of protein, and MPAs help keep fish populations flourishing.

A Biblical Perspective

Have you ever visited the ocean? When you wade into the waves, you are stepping into a body of water that covers most of the earth. It's almost bigger than our minds can comprehend! Just being there with our toes in the water can remind us of other realities too big to fully understand—God, eternity, heaven, love. But we can experience the joys of the ocean without fully appreciating its size, just like we can experience the love of God without fully understanding how He works. It is enough to sink our feet into the sand and feel God's presence.

Our Duty to Others and the Earth

The world is full of people and God loves them all, even those who dump their trash on the ground He created.

Many people toss garbage out of their windows as they drive or drop food wrappers on the ground as they walk. These things happen when people don't think about how this sacred earth was created by a holy God. It's incredibly disrespectful, but we aren't called to punish others for littering. We can pick up the mess of others because we love God and respect His handiwork. By cleaning up after others, we serve them in a way they may never know about or appreciate. It also gives us a chance to love others and the earth in unselfish ways, just like God loves us.

How would you feel if someone dumped their trash on something you created?

Believe it or not, there's a bigger problem than people dropping their trash on the ground. It's called negligence, and it's something that even people who put their trash in bins can be guilty of. Negligence is when someone doesn't follow through on their responsibilities because they either don't care about, or don't realize, the consequences.

What happens to trash after it goes in the bin? Garbage trucks pick it up and take it to a landfill, where it gets covered up but doesn't disappear. Some of the trash will likely escape into waterways and land in the ocean even though we tried to properly throw it away. So how do we keep

trash out of places it shouldn't go? One idea is to make less trash. Ask yourself if you need something before getting it. If you do need something, try to get something reusable (like a glass plate) instead of something designed to be used once (like a paper plate). The other solution is to look for new ways to clean up the mess we've made. As Christians, we need to follow through on the responsibility God gave us to care for the earth. God gave us this beautiful place to live to help us see His glory.

The Remarkable Ocean

Like all parts of nature, the ocean was designed by God and answers His commands. He created the ocean to be moved and stirred by the forces of the sun, moon, air pressure, and wind. The way the earth, moon, and sun dance through space does more than give us seasons. This dance changes the air pressure all around our planet, affecting the tides, the currents, and the spinning parts of the ocean known as gyres.

Like a finely tuned alive and active machine, God set it all in

The Pacific viperfish lives around five thousand feet below the waves but swims up near the surface each night to hunt. This little fish is less than a foot long, but it has a bioluminescent (glowing) belly and fangs that stick out from its bottom jaw to go higher than its eyes. To hunt, the viperfish unhinges its jaw to capture its prey, and its teeth act like the bars of a jail cell.

motion in the earliest days of creation. He set the moon to revolve around the earth. He tilted the earth in relation to the sun. He plotted the path the earth takes around the sun. Together, these different forces work together to give us the wind and waves.

It's so utterly remarkable that during His time on earth, Jesus held the wind and waves at His command. Only a God-man could do that. Matthew 8:27 exclaims, "What sort of man is this, that even winds and sea obey him?" When Jesus stilled the storm, it led the disciples to recognize Him as the Christ. We, too, can see His power and authority in the magnitude and mystery of the ocean.

The Mysterious Ocean

Though it's getting a lot of attention in the news, the ocean is still widely unexplored. We still have more than 80 percent of the ocean to explore and map.[10] People talk about space as the last frontier, but we have many mysteries to discover and unfold about the great blue water basins right here on our own planet.

As it says in Psalm 104:25: "Here is the sea, great and wide, which teems with creatures innumerable, living things both small and great." The depths of the underworld in the Atlantic, Pacific, and Indian Oceans are suspenseful settings of deep darkness and hidden creatures: giant squids, glowing fish, bizarre and enormous marine mammals. The mystery of the ocean draws us and begs us to explore.

As humans explore every corner of the planet, we need to do so with kindness, awe, and wonder. God invites us to learn more about the works of His hands, but never just for us to make money or to do it in ways that are harmful. As Christians, we need to lead with God-sized wisdom to know what explorations are good for the ocean.

HOW YOU CAN MAKE A DIFFERENCE

FOLLOW THE FOUR RS: REFUSE, REDUCE, REUSE, RECYCLE

It's estimated that 17.6 billion pounds of plastic—and possibly up to 12.7 million metric tons—make it into our oceans every year. This is like dumping a garbage truck full of plastic into our oceans each minute.[11] Every person has a role to play in preventing more trash from entering the ocean, and it starts with our daily habits.

Refuse single-use plastic

- Stop using plastic things that only get used once. These are called "single-use plastics." We're talking about straws, plastic spoons (and forks and knives), paper coffee cups, plastic water bottles, and plastic bags. Marine wildlife can get caught in the straps of plastic bags, and sea turtles often mistake floating plastic bags for jellyfish (their favorite snacks!) and try to eat them.
- Buy a travel-size carrying pack of reusable utensils for your lunch bag.
- Ditch plastic straws. Straws can choke and impale the soft tissue of marine animals. Keep a reusable straw handy if needed. Or be extreme and just sip from your cup!
- Food packaging is one of the most common forms of litter found during the Ocean Conservancy's cleanups.[12] Bring your own reusable bags to the grocery store or farmers markets and avoid food prewrapped in plastic.

Reuse and recycle

- Host clothing swaps or yard sales with your friends or with your community. Your "trash" may be a new treasure for a friend!
- Learn your area's recycling rules and continue to check your community's recycling list, as it can change. Recycle everything you can't reduce or refuse if it's on the list.

Reduce

- When you can't refuse, reuse, or recycle, at least try to reduce wherever you can.

USE PLASTIC ALTERNATIVES

As we refuse, reuse, reduce, and recycle, we also need to look into products that don't use so much plastic, which stays on the planet for hundreds of years. There are products in the works that are biodegradable and more eco-friendly, and we should support them where we can.

Cleaning products

- Cleaning products are mostly made up of water. Try brands that come in dissolvable tablets and reusable bottles.

Shampoo and conditioner bars

- To reduce plastic from our beauty and skincare products, try shampoo, conditioner, and bodywash bars by brands like Humankind, Chagrin Valley Soap, or others to find one that works well for you.

Microfiber-free dish cloths

- Choose bamboo-fiber cloths over microfiber cloths or disposable paper towels. They are safe to wash and come from abundant and fast-growing bamboo plants.

LEAD OR JOIN OCEAN CLEANUPS

Cleaning up the great garbage patches in our ocean's gyres seems insurmountable, but there are mega projects underway to attempt to clean it, like the Dutch floating trash collector that was sent into the Pacific Garbage Patch from San Francisco. But the best, most cost-effective thing individuals can do right now is prevent any more plastic trash from entering the ocean.

Coastal cleanups

- Litter on our streets and beaches and in our rivers and streams can become marine debris. Subscribe to NOAA's online monthly newsletter to receive updates on cleanups that may be happening near you.
- When you visit a beach, bring a recycled trash bag with you to pick up litter and leave the area better than when you found it.
- Challenge yourself to cut out waste altogether. Think about the things you use and ask yourself if you need something and how much use you can get out of it. Check out zero waste guides online and Instagram handles with endless creative zero waste tips.

SUPPORT OCEAN NONPROFITS AND INTERNATIONAL PROGRAMS

Check out these organizations to see how you can help

- **Oceana** is focused entirely on ocean conservation. It works to create MPAs, it's already protected more than four million square miles of ocean, and it works to help endangered marine species like the North Atlantic right whale.
- The **Ocean Conservancy** is a group dedicated to protecting marine habitats, promoting sustainable fisheries, and reducing human impacts on the ocean. It also leads yearly beach cleanups.

CHAPTER ELEVEN

THE POLES AND GLOBAL CLIMATE
Our Planet's Future

*From whose womb did the ice come forth, and
who has given birth to the frost of heaven?*

JOB 38:29

What images come to mind when you think about the earth's poles? Maybe you think about polar bears (at the north) and penguins (at the south) and jolly toy-making elves (in stories, anyway). The snowy landscape and the animals who live there can teach us a lot about God.

Vast, open spaces of white snow gleam at the touch of the sun's light, shining like the sinless perfection Jesus gave us at the cross. Narwhals'

The horn of a narwhal is actually a tusk, or huge tooth. Although they are usually shown with only one horn, some narwhals have two!

horns emerge out of cracks in the ice when they come up for air and arctic foxes scurry and jump headfirst into pillowy snow, both finding what they need in what was hidden. The blizzards are an untamed force, and the ice is a strong fortress.

The frozen poles may seem like they belong to a different planet, but they are intimately intertwined with our ordinary lives, down to the wind we feel on our skin. Most of us don't live anywhere near the earth's poles, but wherever we live, we are connected to the polar realms

WHAT ARE FOSSIL FUELS AND GREENHOUSE GASES?

Fossil fuels are the buried bits of decayed plants and animals (whose bodies contain carbon) that have been heated and pressurized in the earth over millennia. In fact, the word *fossil* comes from the Latin *fossilis*, which means "dug up." By burning fossil fuels like coal, oil, and natural gas over centuries, we've raised the levels of heat-trapping (greenhouse) gases in the atmosphere. Greenhouse gases act by forming a "blanket" around the earth, warming the planet. Without greenhouse gases— like carbon dioxide, methane, and water vapor—our planet would be frozen and unsuitable for life. They're good and necessary—in the right amounts.

by the climate. There's a global consensus: 97 percent of scientists agree that the earth's climate is changing at an unnatural rate, largely due to our use of fossil fuels and the trapping of greenhouse gases in the atmosphere, and we are feeling the changes at home.[1]

Carbon Emissions and Fossil Fuels

Carbon dioxide and methane enter the air through cars, trains, planes, boats, factories, farming practices, and deforestation. The Industrial Revolution and use of fossil fuels advanced medicine, gave us electricity, allowed us to travel to new places, and so much more. But we've learned that carbon emissions come at a cost.

The planet has a natural way of cycling and balancing carbon: it's captured in plants and trees during photosynthesis, animals take it up by eating the plants, and it eventually returns to the ground as organic matter. (A similar thing happens between the atmosphere and the ocean.) Carbon *gradually* returns to the air through natural leakage from the crust and volcanic activity (which accounts for a teeny-tiny 1 percent of carbon emissions).

However, humans are taking carbon from the ground in

The Industrial Revolution in a nutshell: This was the time of transition from the late 18th century into the 1900s, where things that were previously made by hand started being made more quickly and efficiently in factories. Previously small towns grew large almost overnight as people moved in so they could work at the factories. Just about every part of society (along with the environment) was changed in some way by the Industrial Revolution.

the form of fossil fuels and injecting it into the atmosphere at a level the natural world has never handled before. As Dr. Katharine Hayhoe, a devoted Christian and renowned climate scientist, says, "God's creation is . . . running a fever."[2] The aches and pains show up as melting ice sheets and rising sea levels, plus an increase in heat waves, droughts, storm intensity, flooding, and forest fires worldwide.

The Impacts on Nature and Humans

Satellites reveal the shrinking ice sheets of the Arctic. Ice levels naturally go up and down with the seasons, but summer ice in the Arctic is shrinking more than 13 percent each decade.[3] Summer ice is already naturally lower (because summers are warmer and there's more sunshine to melt ice), but there is less and less ice during the summer each year. Where does all the melted ice go? It shows up in our rising sea levels, which is a major problem

for cities and communities whose buildings and homes are right on the coast.

And there is another problem. The vast, white surfaces of snow and ice in the polar areas help cool the earth by reflecting the sun's energy back into space. As we lose more ice cover at the poles, the white surface area is replaced by dark ocean waters. You know how black asphalt roads get really hot on sunny summer days? Without ice to reflect the sun's energy back into space, the ocean warms up like those dark roads. The warmer oceans melt more of the ice and the cycle gets worse and worse around the globe. When you add in the rate of deforestation, things look pretty bad. Remember, trees are one of our greatest means of absorbing carbon naturally from the air.

Other impacts—to our water supply, crop growth, and local temperatures—are already being witnessed and felt. The past decade was the hottest recorded in history.[4] Heat waves continue to climb in degree and days, and they're not just discomforting but deadly, especially for people without shelter or air-conditioning.

Extreme weather events continually warn us where we are heading—in just half a decade, a record-breaking five Atlantic hurricanes reached a Category 5 level. Our warming climate has worsened wildfires from Australia to California, threatening homes and vital habitats. Climate change increases the severity of existing problems like water scarcity, biodiversity loss, ocean acidification, coral bleaching, and low crop-production yields. It turns up the dial on almost every environmental problem.

A hotter planet affects our health too. Warmer temperatures provide better breeding grounds for different diseases. Illnesses carried by pests like mosquitoes and ticks (West Nile virus, Lyme disease, and dengue fever) are on the rise in North America. Water-borne diseases like cholera are also on the rise, as flooding and storm damage cause sewage issues and water contamination.

The Greenhouse Effect

NATURAL GREENHOUSE EFFECT

HUMAN GREENHOUSE EFFECT

SOLAR RADIATION

MORE HEAT ESCAPES INTO SPACE

LESS HEAT ESCAPES INTO SPACE

GREENHOUSE GASES

ATMOSPHERE

MORE GREENHOUSE GASES

CO_2

CH_4

N_2O

Fossil Fuel Extraction: Risky Business

Even without the changes caused by a warming world, the ways we dig up and move fossil fuels around are environmentally risky and often unsafe for workers. The pristine Arctic National Wildlife Refuge (ANWR) is the largest wilderness area in the US. It is home to indigenous tribes—the people who originally lived there before groups from other countries moved in and took over—is a breeding ground for polar bears and caribou, and is a habitat for numerous other species, including over two hundred types of migratory birds.[5] ANWR is threatened by oil industry efforts to take away protections and open the refuge to drilling.

Oil

The Keystone XL Pipeline project planned to carry oil 1,200 miles from Alberta, Canada, to Nebraska in the US. After a drawn-out battle in the courts lasting over a decade, it was finally shut down in 2021, but similar pipeline projects are still in the works. Anytime we pump oil out of the ground and move it from one place to another, there's the risk that something will go wrong.

Oil leaks and spills are a constant threat on land and off our

The greenhouse effect is the natural warming of the earth's surface and atmosphere that results from the presence of carbon dioxide, methane, water vapor, and other gases or aerosols. Like a greenhouse, this radiating heat gets trapped in our atmosphere because certain gases allow sunlight to enter while blocking the heat from escaping. Humans have added to this greenhouse effect and messed with the natural level of greenhouse gases in the atmosphere.

coasts. In 1989, the *Exxon Valdez* oil tanker spilled millions of gallons of crude oil off Alaska's coast and covered the Prince William Sound and miles of coastline in a gooey, oily mess. Sea otters, sea turtles, pelicans, dolphins, whales, and many other marine creatures became coated in the oil or ate it. As you can imagine, it wasn't good for them, and countless animals died. It was the largest oil spill in history . . . until the *Deepwater Horizon*'s oil spill in 2010.

Sadly, oil spills happen all over the world, all the time, at varying degrees of severity.

Fracking

Hydraulic fracking is a newer method that drills into the earth and shoots high-pressure liquid into shale rock, breaking open cracks to pump out gas and oil. In the US, it has led to an increase in homegrown oil production and helped lower gas prices. But fracking uses a lot of water and can contaminate local water sources. Plus, we're still researching whether it is creating environmental issues with earthquakes and tremors.[6]

A Way Forward

One of the first things you can do to help the poles and our global climate is figure out your family's carbon footprint (the amount of carbon you are helping put into the atmosphere). This will tell you where most of your family's personal greenhouse gases are coming from and where you can make the biggest difference by changing things. There are many online tools available (like the EPA's online calculator) that will calculate your carbon footprint for you.

Renewable Energy

For a long time—since the Industrial Revolution, in fact—we've depended on fossil fuels to make electricity and provide for a more technologically advanced society. But fossil fuels aren't the way forward anymore. It costs more money (not to mention the cost to the earth) for energy companies to drill in new places and transport the coal and oil to places where they can turn them into useable fuel. It makes better sense financially for energy companies to invest in cleaner, safer ways to make electricity.

Clean energy, or renewable energy, comes from largely carbon-free sources, which are naturally replenished—like sunlight, wind, water, and geothermal heat (literally the heat that exists inside the earth). These options are promising and constantly improving and growing. Investing in, buying, and making clean energy available for all countries is a worthy goal. (Remember William Kamkwamba's story?) And by pursuing renewable energy, the energy companies will create new jobs and businesses that are better for people and the planet. This will require a wise transition that helps workers in the fossil fuel energy shift to renewable energy skills and jobs. It's time to make this happen!

Our Planet's Natural Solution

Switching to renewable energy sources is half of the solution to global warming. It can stop the greenhouse gases we are currently

adding to the atmosphere, but what do we do about the carbon dioxide that's already up there? The answer is in the planet itself.

The earth has natural ways to soak up carbon—wetlands, trees, plants, grass, seagrass, seaweed, kelp, and soil. These are all referred to as "carbon sinks." Vegetation captures carbon through photosynthesis, and microbes and fungi help break plants down, trapping the carbon in the soil. Reforesting the earth, restoring wetlands, protecting our kelp forests and seagrass beds, and switching to regenerative agriculture were solutions in earlier chapters, and now they're also the answer to the world's biggest challenge: climate change. Be encouraged: We can do this! You can do this! A planet of clear blues and deep greens is possible for you and for the kids of the future.

A Biblical Perspective

God designed every little part of our planet to connect to every other little part in its large climate system, from pole to pole. What we do at home changes what happens at the poles and around the world. Here's the thing: it's the financially poorer communities, and developing countries especially, who suffer the most from everyone's lifestyle choices surrounding fossil fuel use.

Imagine if some billionaire bought the house next to you and threw a party every week. The parties are loud, the guests throw their trash into your yard, and you can't do anything to stop them because your billionaire neighbors have more power in town. You'd like to move, but no one else is going to buy your house, and you couldn't afford a new house anyway. It isn't exactly fair, but it is the way the world works. Unless the billionaire is willing to see how their actions are affecting you, things will probably stay the same or get worse.

That's how it is with the big, rich countries of the world and the financially poorer countries who can't afford to change things for themselves. These countries are suffering the most from climate change—with hurricanes, fires, droughts, and floods—and they have the fewest resources to help their citizens.

No matter how far apart we are in the world, we are responsible for polar ecosystems and communities around the world. If we think we are only responsible for the things that affect us negatively without considering how our actions are affecting others, we are not reflecting God's love to the world very well. As Christians, we can't ignore the consequences of our daily decisions on others. We should be known as the meek who "will inherit the earth" (Matthew 5:5 NIV) and not the "destroyers of the earth" who greatly displease God (Revelation 11:18). Let's reduce our oil consumption and electricity use, take real steps away from fossil fuels, support renewable energy, and work to make the world a healthier place together.

Consult Your Conscience

There are so many reasons—air pollution, water quality, oil drilling risks and disasters—to make changes toward clean energy. As you remember everything you read in this book, think about what stands out and what changes you can make. Don't change your actions because you are scared the world is going to end tomorrow (it probably won't); change them because you know it's the right thing to do. Fear is a terrible long-term motivator. Listening to the Spirit and doing what is right is way better because it comes from love for God and His world.

The Redemption of Creation

Romans 8:22 tells us that creation is part of God's ultimate redemption plan: "The whole creation has been groaning together in the pains of childbirth until now." We see those groans in the environmental disasters, disease outbreaks, diminishing polar ice, famines, and floods. Jesus came to earth

to heal and restore. He gave sight to the blind and helped the lame to walk again. But Jesus came for more than just people. He came to restore ALL of creation to Himself!

The world's redemption doesn't need to wait until Jesus's second coming. Since God's Spirit dwells in us right now, we can start restoring the world today!

When Jesus comes back at the second coming, creation will go back to the way God originally made it to be. This is our hope. This is the final act of the gospel. The renewing Spirit will reach every ounce of the cosmos, from galaxy to galaxy, and from pole to pole. Creation's final, perfect redemption will be a knee-bending revealing of the glory of the Lord. It's like God is stepping back to the moment He finished creation and declaring it not just good, but great.

For now, our calling is to become restorers of our land and communities. The world needs to be encouraged to hope and believe in a God who is actively saving and redeeming. We have the chance, right now, when the news is full of environmental problems and fear is running high, to step out in faith and bring healing to a broken world.

The ways we work toward restoring the earth today point to the future when Jesus will restore everything perfectly. Our future heaven on earth will be just as God planned, and all of creation can flourish without pain, corruption, or greed. No one will go hungry, and there will be no death. Instead, all of us, in our own ways, will find worship in all we do.

HOW YOU CAN MAKE A DIFFERENCE

REDUCE YOUR CARBON FOOTPRINT AT HOME

Most of the energy we use happens in our homes. Every light we leave on after leaving the room takes power. Small changes and energy-saving projects at home can cut carbon emissions.

Have your family conduct a home energy audit

💧 Many power companies offer home energy audits that figure out how much energy you are using. They can also make suggestions on how to use energy more efficiently to prevent waste.

Dress warm in the winter and cool in the summer

💧 Instead of asking your caregivers to warm or cool the house, dress for the temperature it is. The Department of Energy (DOE) advises keeping the difference between the indoor and outdoor temperatures as small as possible.[7] Pile on the blankets and sweaters in the winter!

Reduce energy use from appliances

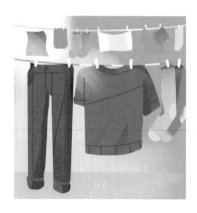

💧 Dry laundry on a rack or clothesline instead of in the dryer.

💧 Turn off lights, hit the switch on power strips, and unplug electronics when not in use.

- Open windows or use a fan for as long as possible before turning on the AC.

Stock up on fruits, vegetables, and legumes

- Believe it or not, cutting back on meat is a major help! Meat-heavy American diets make up for one-fifth of global emissions.[8] Try out a Beyond Burger or other meat alternatives!
- Cows pass loads of methane gas into the air, bless their hearts. Cattle ranching in places like Brazil is causing massive deforestation, and we need those trees to soak up carbon dioxide. The personal sacrifice of reducing your hamburger count is worth it.

Practice climate-friendly lawn management

- Plant trees, shrubs, and other native plants in your yard. All plants remove carbon dioxide from the air and store it in their roots, leaves, wood, and stems.
- Fruit trees and berry bushes offer fresh food to harvest right from your yard. It's wholesome, fun, and helpful for the climate!
- According to the US Forest Service, trees remove 10 to 20 percent of the annual fossil fuel emissions in the US.[9] We have natural carbon capturers in our trees!

THINK ABOUT YOUR TRANSPORTATION CHOICES TO LOWER YOUR CARBON FOOTPRINT

We are often on the move between home, errands, and school. Going from one place to another is a big part of our lives, and it's a gift. We can pick up habits that reduce emissions and lead by example for others to follow.

Rethink your dream car

- Many car manufacturers are turning toward electric vehicles—EVs—as a way to take care of their customers and the planet.

- EVs always reduce greenhouse gas emissions, especially when the electricity source is renewable, and they are increasingly more feasible and affordable.

- If you could design the perfect EV, what would it be like? What color would it be? How about a convertible? Also think about all the ways you could make it better for the planet!

Bike often

- Biking is a healthy, active, zero-emissions alternative to driving. With a caregiver's permission, bike to school, sports practice, and other close destinations.

Use public transportation or carpool

- Carpool with your friends and classmates to school, sporting events, and other errands. Fewer cars on the road mean less emissions.

- Take the bus, subway, metro, or rail when possible.

RESEARCH RENEWABLE ENERGY OPTIONS TO LOWER YOUR CARBON FOOTPRINT

All our energy use at home can contribute to greenhouse gas emissions unless we choose to make the switch to renewables. The US electricity supply is separated into conventional energy (coal, nuclear, oil, and natural gas) and renewable energy or green power (sources that are continually replenished over time without becoming depleted).

What would it look like to switch to green power in your home?

- Electricity production accounts for 25 percent of greenhouse gas emissions globally.[10]
- Some major renewable options with promising growth and availability are solar power, wind energy, and geothermal energy.
- Ask your caregivers to install solar panels at your home. There may be local, state, and federal incentives for solar power in your region. Lead by example in your neighborhood with renewable generation right on your property.

ADVOCATE TO SPEED UP THE TRANSITION TO RENEWABLE ENERGY

While our personal energy habits matter, the energy system at large is like a giant machine that's been running off fossil fuels for decades. There are challenges to overcome in transitioning from the oil reserves to renewable sources, but we can fight for a just and prompt transition to clean energy.

Write a letter to your state representative to encourage them to uphold renewable energy bills

- Government officials love hearing from the people they represent. That includes you! Write out why you think renewable energy is so important. Include some ideas on programs they can support.
- If you have extra time, draw a picture to include as well. Maybe solar panels on your roof or an electric bus.

Talk about climate change issues

- Watch documentaries or listen to podcasts with friends and family and discuss what you think together. Some podcasts to check out: *The Big Melt, Wow in the World,* and *Fun Kids Science Weekly,* which all have episodes based around climate change.
- Check out Dr. Katharine Hayhoe's "Global Weirding" YouTube channel for clear and helpful insights into the questions and issues. Become informed so you'll be more equipped to share and help others process and make changes too.

CHECK OUT THE NATIONAL OCEAN SERVICE

The National Oceanic and Atmospheric Administration (NOAA), which is also known as the National Ocean Service, does a lot of great work for the oceans.

See what's happening with oil spill cleanups

- The US Coast Guard is the main authority for cleaning up oil spills in the United States with the scientific advice and support of NOAA. Follow NOAA's "Eyes in the Sky Surveilling for Pollution" project, which publishes oil spills in near–real time online.
- Cleaning oil from an environment requires professional training and skill because people can end up causing additional damage even when trying to help. As much as you may want to help clean up an oil spill, it's a job better left to the professionals.

Check out the Student Opportunities page of NOAA

- Grab a caregiver and head over to NOAA's Student Opportunities webpage at www.noaa.gov/education/opportunities/students to see all the things you can participate in right now. There are virtual science fairs, scholarship opportunities, art contests, and more!

SUPPORT NONPROFITS WORKING ON CLIMATE ACTION

The following organizations are doing good work in climate action:

- World Relief focuses on clean energy, community building, and helping climate refugees (communities who were forced out of their homes by sea level rise, drought, and other climate-related crises).
- Convoy of Hope works in disaster relief and preparedness.
- World Renew aids in natural disaster response, clean energy, and food insecurity with a focus on family-centered community development.
- To get involved in faith-based climate policy advocacy, check out the Evangelical Environmental Network and YECA (Young Evangelicals For Climate Action).

GLOSSARY

Air Pollution: When the mix of life-sustaining gases gets messed up or mixed with toxic elements. This is terrible for ecosystems and human health.

Aquifer: An underground layer of porous (hole-filled) rock that acts like a sponge, allowing water in the ground to move up through saturated rock and sediment.

Bioaccumulation: When toxic chemicals build up in living organisms.

Biodiversity: Refers to the great variety of life on earth, and describes the number of different species (plant, animal, and fungus) in a community, ecosystem, or biome.

Brackish: A mix of fresh and salty water.

Clean Air Act (CAA): A group of laws passed in 1970 that allowed the US government to regulate air pollution emissions from sources like vehicles, power plants, and factories. It also addressed chemical pollutants that are damaging the atmosphere's ozone layer, and it aimed to reduce acid rain and improve air quality and visibility.

Clean Water Act (CWA): A group of laws passed in 1972 that made it unlawful to dump pollutants into rivers, streams, and other bodies of water without a permit. The CWA also regulates quality standards for surface waters.

Confined animal feeding operations (CAFO): An industrial agricultural practice where livestock animals (like cows, pigs, and chickens) live in cramped conditions. These animals are especially susceptible to the spread of disease.

Decaying material: Anything that is decomposing and adding good material and nutrients back into the soil, such as rotting fruits and vegetables or animals who have died.

Deforestation: When forests disappear because we don't replant trees fast enough to replace them.

Ecosystem: An interconnected community made up of living things (animals and organisms) and their non-living environment, working together as a unit. Different areas of the planet have completely different kinds of ecosystems.

Endangered Species Act (ESA): A group of laws passed in 1973 that protects threatened species and their habitats by requiring development projects to get permits when the project may impact an endangered species. The ESA also stops people from hunting at-risk species. This group of laws has an impressive success rate—99 percent of species protected under it have avoided extinction! It's brought back many species from the brink of extinction, including the bald eagle, peregrine falcon, gray wolf, and grizzly bear.

Estuary: A partially enclosed body of water where a river meets the sea, creating a mixture of fresh and salt water.

Fen: a type of wetland that is made of low land that's either completely or partly covered with water. The soil is peaty—which means it's wet, spongy, and filled with decaying plants—and there are often reeds and similar plants growing in the area.

Food chain: One animal eats another, then another animal eats that one, and so on. Humans tend to be at the top of the food chain because we eat so many plants and animals.

Food web: Like a food chain, but it recognizes that even when animals aren't eating each other directly, they can impact the diets of other animals. Humans don't eat bees, but we do eat the honey that bees make, so we're connected via the food web.

Haecceity: The "thisness" of any one thing. It's what makes your favorite stuffed animal different from every other similar stuffed animal.

Industrial agriculture: Farms that are owned and worked by big companies instead of by small families. These big companies use technology to grow the most food per square foot possible and often only grow one type of crop instead of lots of different ones.

Invasive species: Plants and animals that are plopped into an ecosystem from somewhere else, often by humans, and harm the plants and animals that were there first.

Light pollution: Artificial (man-made) light that blocks our view of the night sky. It can change our sleeping habits, trick animals into hibernating and eating at the wrong times, and mess with bird migrations.

Megafauna: Big animals from around the world, like rhinoceroses, elephants, pandas, and leopards.

Minimalism: Only buying the things you need.

Monsoon: A seasonal change in the direction of a region's strongest winds. They always blow from cold to warm regions. When the winds are moving from land to the ocean, the weather in a region is extremely dry. When the winds blow from the ocean to the land, the region has heavy rainfall.

Mountaintop removal: Blowing up mountaintops to get to the rocks buried underneath. This method is mainly used to mine coal. It doesn't only destroy the beauty of the mountains; millions of tons of rock, sand, and coal debris (tiny bits) from the explosions are dumped in the valleys and end up polluting waterways and the atmosphere. This mining practice has caused a lot of arguments in the central Appalachian Mountains, where communities near the mines suffer from an increase in heart diseases, lung cancer, and birth defects.

Overexploitation: When people hunt and harvest wildlife faster than the population of that wildlife can reproduce.

Overfishing: When people take so many of one kind of fish out of a body of water that it throws off the balance of the ecosystem.

Particulate matter: A mixture of solid particles and air droplets light enough to float in the air. This includes dust, pollen, soot, or smoke, but the more troubling varieties are made up of chemicals from power plants and automobiles.

Photosynthesis: The process in which plants and other organisms capture carbon dioxide and sunlight to produce oxygen and chemical energy in the form of sugar (plant food!).

Plogging: Picking up litter as you go for a run. The word is a mashup of the Swedish words *plocka upp* (which means "pick up") and *jogga* (which means "jog").

Pollinator: Anything that helps carry pollen from one part of a flower, bush, or tree to another to allow that plant to produce fruits, seeds, and young plants.

Reservoir: A place to keep water for when you need it.

Soil erosion: When soil washes away or turns into plain old dirt due to a lack of nutrients.

Symbiotic relationship: When two different things work together in ways that help them both.

Tectonic plates: Different sections of the earth's crust and upper mantle that float on top of the liquid magma (melted rock) near the earth's core.

Upcycle: Creatively reusing the things you no longer need in order to give them a new life as something else.

Zoonotic: The kind of disease that can jump from animals living in the wild to animals on farms to people. A few examples of zoonotic diseases include Ebola, West Nile virus, and Lyme disease.

NOTES

Chapter 1: Fresh Water

1. "1 in 3 People Globally Do Not Have Access to Safe Drinking Water—UNICEF, WHO," World Health Organization, June 18, 2019, https://www.who.int/news/item/18-06-2019-1-in-3 -people-globally-do-not-have-access-to-safe-drinking-water -unicef-who.

2. "Poverty Status in the Past Twelve Months," American Community Survey, 2016, United States Census Bureau, accessed March, 27, 2022, https://data.census.gov/cedsci/table?q=flint%20 michigan%202016%20poverty&tid=ACSST1Y2016.S1701.

3. Melissa Denchak, "Flint Water Crisis: Everything You Need to Know," NRDC.org, November 8, 2018, https://www.nrdc.org /stories/flint-water-crisis-everything-you-need-know.

4. Meera Subramanian, "India's Terrifying Water Crisis," *New York Times*, July 15, 2019, https://www.nytimes.com/2019/07/15 /opinion/india-water-crisis.html.

5. Anthony Acciavatti, "The Ganges Water Crisis," *New York Times*, June 17, 2015, https://www.nytimes.com/2015/06/18/opinion /the-ganges-water-crisis.html?ref=international&_r=0; Simon Scarr, Weiyi Cai, Vinod Kumar, and Alasdair Pal, "The Race to Save the River Ganges," Reuters.com, January 18, 2019, https:// graphics.reuters.com/INDIA-RIVER/010081TW39P/index .html.

Chapter 2: Endangered Species

1. Traci Watson, "86 Percent of Earth's Species Still Unknown?," National Geographic News, August 25, 2011, https://www.nationalgeographic.com/science/article/110824-earths-species-8-7-million-biology-planet-animals-science.

2. Sandra Díaz et al., "Summary for Policymakers of the Global Assessment Report on Biodiversity and Ecosystem Services of the Intergovernmental Science-Policy Platform on Biodiversity and Ecosystem Services," IPBES, 2019, https://ipbes.net/sites/default/files/2020–02/ipbes_global_assessment_report_summary_for_policymakers_en.pdf.

3. Gerardo Ceballos, Paul R. Ehrlich, and Peter H. Raven, "Vertebrates on the Brink as Indicators of Biological Annihilation and the Sixth Mass Extinction," *PNAS* 117, no. 24 (June 2020): 13596–13602, https://www.pnas.org/doi/pdf/10.1073/pnas.1922686117.

4. "*Enhydra lutris*—sea otter," Animal Diversity Web, https://animaldiversity.org/site/accounts/information/Enhydra_lutris.html. Accessed March 25, 2022.

5. Kate Garibaldi, "Sea Otters," Defenders of Wildlife, Accessed September 2021, https://defenders.org/wildlife/sea-otter.

6. "Snow Leopard Range Map," Snow Leopard Conservancy, 2011, https://snowleopardconservancy.org/text/how/range.html; "Action for Snow Leopards," IUCN, August 14, 2020, https://www.iucn.org/news/eastern-europe-and-central-asia/202008/action-snow-leopards.

7. "Ili Pika: *Ochotona iliensis*," IUCN Red List, accessed March 30, 2022, https://www.iucnredlist.org/species/150[50]/45179204#threats.

8. "Threats to African Elephants," World Wildlife Fund, accessed August 26, 2021, https://wwf.panda.org/discover

/knowledge_hub/endangered_species/elephants
/african_elephants/afelephants_threats/?.

9. "Poaching for Rhino Horn," Save the Rhino, accessed August 26, 2021, https://www.savetherhino.org/rhino-info /threats/poaching-rhino-horn/; Dina Fine Maron, "China Legalizes Rhino Horn and Tiger Bone for Medical Purposes," Nationalgeographic.com, October 29, 2018, https://www .nationalgeographic.com/animals/article/wildlife-watch-news -china-rhino-tiger-legal#:~:text=Rhino%20horn%20is%20 made%20from,in%20humans%20from%20either%20product.

10. Muhammad Adnan Shereen, Suliman Khan, Abeer Kazmi, Nadia Bashir, and Rabeea Siddique, "COVID-19 Infection: Emergence, Transmission, and Characteristics of Human Coronaviruses," *Journal of Advanced Research* 24 (July 2020): 91–98, https://doi .org/10.1016/j.jare.2020.03.005.

11. Ping Liu et al., "Are Pangolins the Intermediate Host of the 2019 Novel Coronavirus (SARS-CoV-2)?" *PLOS Pathogens* 16, no. 5 (May 2020): e1008421, https://doi.org/10.1371/journal. ppat.1008421.

12. "Giant Goldfish Problem in US Lake Prompts Warning to Pet Owners," BBC News, July 13, 2021, https://www.bbc.com /news/world-us-canada-57816922.

Chapter 3: Mountains and Minerals

1. Based on information from "Inside the Earth," USGS, https:// pubs.usgs.gov/gip/dynamic/inside.html.

2. Richard Schiffman, "A Troubling Look at the Human Toll of Mountaintop Removal Mining," *Yale Environment 360*, November 21, 2017, https://e360.yale.edu/features/a-troubling-look-at-the -human-toll-of-mountaintop-removal-mining; Sarah Saadoun, "The Coal Mine Next Door: How the US Government's

Deregulation of Mountaintop Removal Threatens Public Health," Human Rights Watch, December 10, 2018, https://www.hrw.org/report/2018/12/10/coal-mine-next-door/how-us-governments-deregulation-mountaintop-removal-threatens.

3. Megan R. Nichols, "5 Ways to Make Mining More Sustainable," Empowering Pumps and Equipment, February 18, 2020, https://empoweringpumps.com/5-ways-to-make-mining-more-sustainable/.

4. "Green Mining," Mission 2016: The Future of Strategic Natural Resources, MIT, 2016, https://web.mit.edu/12.000/www/m2016/finalwebsite/solutions/greenmining.html.

5. Michael Standeaert, "China Wrestles with the Toxic Aftermath of Rare Earth Mining," *Yale Environment 360*, July 2, 2019, https://e360.yale.edu/features/china-wrestles-with-the-toxic-aftermath-of-rare-earth-mining.

6. "Electronics Donation and Recycling," Environmental Protection Agency, accessed August 26, 2021, https://www.epa.gov/recycle/electronics-donation-and-recycling.

7. Based on Science Buddies activity "Model the Rock Cycle with Crayons," https://www.sciencebuddies.org/stem-activities/crayon-rock-cycle#exploremore.

Chapter 4: Air and Sky

1. National Geographic Society, "Light Pollution," *National Geographic*, July 23, 2019, https://www.nationalgeographic.org/article/light-pollution/.

2. "Visibility and Regional Haze," United States Environmental Protection Agency, accessed August 26, 2021, https://www.epa.gov/visibility.

3. United Nations Environment Programme, "Towards a Pollution-Free Planet: Background Report," UN Environment

Assembly, September 2017, https://wedocs.unep.org/bitstream /handle/20.500.118²²/21800/UNEA_towardspollution _long%20version_Web.pdf?sequence=1&isAllowed=y.

4. Rachel M. Shaffer, Magali N. Blango, Ge Li, Sara D. Adar, Marco Carone, Adam A. Szpiro, Joel D. Kaufman, Timothy V. Larson, Eric B. Larson, Paul K. Crane, and Lianne Sheppard, "Fine Particulate Matter and Dementia Incidence in the Adult Changes in Thought Study," *Environmental Health Perspectives*, Vol. 129, No. 8, Published August 4, 2021, https://ehp.niehs.nih.gov /doi/10.1289/EHP9018.

5. "Air Pollution," WHO, accessed August 26, 2021, https://www .who.int/westernpacific/health-topics/air-pollution?msclkid =c4d0b761aeda11ecb97f6dcdf5c12346.

6. "Air Pollution," WHO.

7. "Air Pollution," WHO.

8. "Air Pollution," WHO.

9. Miranda Green, "EPA Scientists Find Black Communities Disproportionately Hit by Pollution," *The Hill*, February 23, 2018, https://thehill.com/policy/energy-environment/375289-epa-scientists-find-emissions-greater-impact-low-income-communities.

10. Bruce Bekkar, MD; Susan Pacheco, MD; Rupa Basu, PhD; et al, "Association of Air Pollution and Heat Exposure with Preterm Birth, Low Birth Weight, and Stillbirth in the US," *Journal of the American Medical Association*, published June 18, 2020, https:// jamanetwork.com/journals/jamanetworkopen/fullarticle /2767260?utm_source=For_The_Media&utm_medium =referral&utm_campaign=ftm_links&utm_term=061820.

11. James A. Johnstone and Todd E. Dawson, "Climatic context and ecological implications of summer fog decline in the coast redwood region," *Proceedings of the National Academy of Sciences* 107.10 (2010): 4533–4538.

12. Marcel Theroux, "The World's Dirtiest Air," *Unreported World*, April 29, 2018, YouTube video, 23:50, https://youtu.be /kUNuHxrd7Y0.

13. "Frequently Asked Questions (FAQs)," US Energy Information Administration, accessed March 28, 2022, https://www.eia.gov /tools/faqs/faq.php?id=427&t=3.

Chapter 5: Woodlands

1. "12 Days of Conifers: Conifer Trees and How We Study Them," USGS/Western Ecological Research Center (WERC), accessed March 29, 2022, https://www.usgs.gov/news/12-days-conifers -conifer-trees-and-how-we-study-them.

2. "UN Report: Nature's Dangerous Decline 'Unprecedented'; Species Extinction Rates 'Accelerating,'" *Sustainable Development Goals* (blog), UN, May 6, 2019, https://www.un.org /sustainabledevelopment/blog/2019/05/nature-decline -unprecedented-report/.

3. "Yale Experts Explain Healthy Forests," Yale Office of Sustainability, December 16, 2020, https://sustainability.yale .edu/explainers/yale-experts-explain-healthy-forests?utm_source =YaleToday&utm_medium=Email&utm_campaign=YT _YaleToday-Students_12–22–2020.

4. Mikaela Weisse and Elizabeth Dow Goldman, "We Lost a Football Pitch of Primary Rainforest Every 6 Seconds in 2019," World Resources Institute, June 2, 2020, https://www.wri.org /insights/we-lost-football-pitch-primary-rainforest-every-6 -seconds-2019.

5. "Forests and Poverty Reduction," Food and Agriculture Organization of the United Nations, last updated May 15, 2015, http://www.fao.org/forestry/livelihoods/en/.

6. "Deforestation and Forest Degradation," World Wildlife Fund,

accessed August 26, 2021, https://www.worldwildlife.org/threats
/deforestation-and-forest-degradation.

7. Domingos Cardoso et al., "Amazon Plant Diversity Revealed
by a Taxonomically Verified Species List," PNAS 114, no. 40
(September 2017): 10695–10700, https://doi.org/10.1073/pnas
.1706756114.

8. *Encyclopedia Britannica*, s.v. "Amazon Rainforest," accessed August
27, 2021, https://www.britannica.com/place/Amazon-Rainforest.

9. "Deforestation and Forest Degradation," World Wildlife Fund.

10. "What Animals Live in the Amazon? And 8 other Amazon Facts,"
WWF, accessed March 22, 2022, https://www.worldwildlife
.org/stories/what-animals-live-in-the-amazon-and-8-other
-amazon-facts.

11. Gregory S. Cooper, Simon Willcock, and John A. Dearing,
"Regime Shifts Occur Disproportionately Faster in Larger
Ecosystems," *Nature Communications* 11, no. 1175 (March 2020),
https://doi.org/10.1038/s41467-020-15029-x; Fen Montaigne,
"Will Deforestation and Warming Push the Amazon to a Tipping
Point?" *Yale Environment 360*, September 4, 2019, https://e360
.yale.edu/features/will-deforestation-and-warming-push-the
-amazon-to-a-tipping-point; Carlos A. Nobre et al., "Land-use
and Climate Change Risks in the Amazon and the Need of a
Novel Sustainable Development Paradigm," PNAS 113, no. 39
(September 2016): 10759–10768, https://doi.org/10.1073/pnas
.1605516113.

12. Robert Toovey Walker et al., "Avoiding Amazonian Catastrophes:
Prospects for Conservation in the 21st Century," *One Earth*, vol.
1, no. 2 (October 2019): 202–215, https://doi.org/10.1016/j
.oneear.2019.09.009.

13. Tree of Life," Bible Project, accessed August 27, 2021, https://
bibleproject.com/learn/tree-of-life/.

14. Gabrielle Kissinger, Martin Herold, and Veronique De Sy, "Drivers of Deforestation and Forest Degradation: A Synthesis Report for REDD+ Policymakers," Lexeme Consulting, August 2012, https://assets.publishing.service.gov.uk/government/uploads/system/uploads/attachment_data/file/655⁰⁵/6316-drivers-deforestation-report.pdf.

15. "7 Everyday Foods from the Rainforest," Rainforest Alliance, last updated September 16, 2017, https://www.rainforest-alliance.org/articles/7-everyday-foods-from-the-rainforest.

16. "Paper and Paperboard: Material—Specific Data," EPA, last updated January 27, 2022, https://www.epa.gov/facts-and-figures-about-materials-waste-and-recycling/paper-and-paperboard-material-specific-data#:~:text=Approximately%2046%20million%20tons%20of,recycling%20rate%20of%2064.8%20percent.

Chapter 6: Soil

1. "24 Billion Tons of Fertile Land Lost Every Year, Warns UN Chief on World Day to Combat Desertification," *UN News*, June 16, 2019, https://news.un.org/en/story/2019/06/1040561.

2. David Pimentel, "Soil Erosion: A Food and Environmental Threat," *Journal of the Environment, Development and Sustainability*, 8 (February 2006): 119–137, https://doi.org/10.1007/s10668–005–1262–8.

3. "Hunger and Food Insecurity," Food and Agriculture Organization of the UN, accessed March 30, 2022, https://www.fao.org/hunger/en/.

4. "Part 1: Food Security and Nutrition Around the World in 2020," Food and Agriculture Organization of the UN, accessed August 27, 2021, http://www.fao.org/3/ca9692en/online/ca9692en.html#chapter-1_1.

5. Eric Holt-Giménez, Annie Shattuck, Miguel A. Altieri, Hans

Herren, and Steve Gliessman, "We Already Grow Enough Food for 10 Billion People . . . and Still Can't End Hunger," *Journal of Sustainable Agriculture*, vol. 36, no. 6 (July 2012): 595–598, https://doi.org/10.10^{80}/$_{10}$440046.2012.695331.

6. H. Charles J. Godfray et al., "Food Security: The Challenge of Feeding 9 Billion People," *Science*, vol. 327, no. 5967 (January 2010): 812–818, https://doi.org/10.1126/science.1185383.

7. "Food Waste in America in 2021: Statistics and Facts," RTS, accessed August 27, 2021, https://www.rts.com/resources/guides/food-waste-america/.

8. "Grocery Industry Launches New Initiative to Reduce Consumer Confusion on Product Date Labels," Consumer Brands Association, February 15, 2017, https://consumerbrandsassociation.org/posts/grocery-industry-launches-new-initiative-to-reduce-consumer-confusion-on-product-date-labels/.

9. "Composting at Home," United States Environmental Protection Agency, accessed April 1, 2022, https://www.epa.gov/recycle/composting-home.

10. "Composting at Home," United States Environmental Protection Agency.

11. "How Your T-Shirt Can Make a Difference," World Wildlife Fund, accessed April 1, 2022, https://www.worldwildlife.org/videos/how-your-t-shirt-can-make-a-difference.

Chapter 7: Pollinators

1. Simon G. Potts et al., "Summary for Policymakers of the Assessment Report of the Intergovernmental Science-Policy Platform on Biodiversity and Ecosystem Services on Pollinators, Pollination and Food Production" (Bonn, Germany: IPBES, 2016), https://ipbes.net/sites/default/files/spm_deliverable_3a_pollination_20170222.pdf.

2. Jeff Ollerton, Rachael Winfree, and Sam Tarrant, "How Many Flowering Plants Are Pollinated by Animals?" *Oikos* 120, no. 3 (March 2011): 321–326, https://doi.org/10.1111/j.1600–0706 .2010.18644.x.

3. Caspar A. Hallmann et al., "More Than 75 Percent Decline Over 27 Years in Total Flying Insect Biomass in Protected Areas," *PLOS ONE* 12, no. 10 (October 2017): e0185809, https://doi .org/10.1371/journal.pone.0185809.

4. Francisco Sánchez-Bayo and Kris A. G. Wyckhuys, "Worldwide Decline of the Entomofauna: A Review of Its Drivers," *Biological Conservation* 232 (April 2019): 8–27, https://doi.org/10.1016/j .biocon.2019.01.020.

5. Jamie Ellis, "The Honey Bee Crisis," *Outlooks on Pest Management* 23, no. 1 (February 2012): 35–40,https://doi.org/10.1564/22feb10.

6. Laura A. Burkle, John C. Marlin, and Tiffany M. Knight, "Plant-Pollinator Interactions over 120 Years: Loss of Species, Co-Occurrence, and Function," *Science*, February 28, 2013, Vol. 339, Issue 6127, pp. 1611–15, https://www.science.org/lookup /doi/10.1126/science.1232728.

7. Sarina Jepsen et al., "Conservation Status and Ecology of Monarchs in the United States" (Arlington, VA and Portland, OR: NatureServe and the Xerces Society, 2015), https://www .xerces.org/sites/default/files/2018–05/15–016_01_XercesSoc _Conservation-Status-Ecology-Monarch-US-web.pdf.

8. "Saving the Monarch Butterfly," Center for Biological Diversity, accessed April 1, 2022, https://www.biologicaldiversity.org species/invertebrates/monarch_butterfly/.

9. "Migratory Monarch Butterfly Now Endangered—IUCN Red List," IUCN.org, accessed August 16, 2022, https://www.iucn. org/press-release/202207/migratory-monarch-butterfly-now -endangered-iucn-red-list.

10. "Bat Pollination," US Forest Service, accessed August 27, 2021, https://www.fs.fed.us/wildflowers/pollinators/animals/bats.shtml.

11. Christian Schwägerl, "What's Causing the Sharp Decline in Insects, and Why It Matters," *Yale Environment 360*, July 6, 2016, https://e360.yale.edu/features/insect_numbers_declining _why_it_matters.

12. Susannah B. Lerman, Alexandra R. Contosta, Joan Milam, and Christofer Bang, "To Mow or to Mow Less: Lawn Mowing Frequency Affects Bee Abundance and Diversity in Suburban Yards," *Biological Conservation*, vol. 221 (May 2018): 160–174, https://doi.org/10.1016/j.biocon.2018.01.025.

13. "Monarch Waystation Program," Monarch Watch, accessed August 27, 2021, https://www.monarchwatch.org/waystations/.

14. Leonard Perry, "Beneficial Nematodes," University of Vermont, Department of Plant and Soil Science, accessed August 27, 2021, https://pss.uvm.edu/ppp/articles/nemat.html.

Chapter 8: Wetlands

1. Natural Resources Conservation Service, "Restoring America's Wetlands: A Private Lands Conservation Success Story," USDA, accessed August 27, 2021, https://www.nrcs.usda.gov/Internet /FSE_DOCUMENTS/stelprdb1045079.pdf.

2. "Wetlands Disappearing Three Times Faster Than Forests," UN Climate Change News, October 1, 2018, https://unfccc.int/news /wetlands-disappearing-three-times-faster-than-forests.

3. "Wetlands Disappearing Three Times Faster Than Forests," UN Climate Change News.

4. "Coastal Wetland Habitat," National Oceanic and Atmospheric Administration, last updated February 4, 2022, https://www .fisheries.noaa.gov/national/habitat-conservation/coastal-wetlands -too-valuable-lose.

5. "Call for an Ambitious Global Biodiversity Framework on World Wetlands Day 2020," IUCN, January 31, 2020, https://www.iucn.org/news/water/202001/call-ambitious-global-biodiversity-framework-world-wetlands-day-2020.

Chapter 9: Coral Reefs

1. "Shallow Coral Reef Habitat," National Oceanic and Atmospheric Administration, last updated February 4, 2022, https://www.fisheries.noaa.gov/national/habitat-conservation/shallow-coral-reef-habitat.

2. "Shallow Coral Reef Habitat," NOAA Fisheries, last updated February 4, 2022, https://www.fisheries.noaa.gov/national/habitat-conservation/shallow-coral-reef-habitat.

3. "Coral Reef Ecosystems," National Oceanic and Atmospheric Administration, last updated February 1, 2019, https://www.noaa.gov/education/resource-collections/marine-life/coral-reef-ecosystems.

4. Terry P. Hughes et al., "Ecological Memory Modifies the Cumulative Impact of Recurrent Climate Extremes," *Nature Climate Change* 9 (2019): 40–43, https://doi.org/10.1038/s41558-018-0351-2; Andreas Dietzel, Michael Bode, Sean R. Connolly, and Terry P. Hughes, "Long-Term Shifts in the Colony Size Structure of Coral Populations Along the Great Barrier Reef," *Proceedings of the Royal Society B: Biological Sciences* 287, no. 1936 (October 2020), https://doi.org/10.1098/rspb.2020.1432.

5. "Coral Reef Ecosystems," National Oceanic and Atmospheric Administration.

6. "Coral Reef Ecosystems," National Oceanic and Atmospheric Administration.

7. Robert Brumbaugh, "Healthy Coral Reefs Are Good for Tourism—And Tourism Can Be Good for Reefs," World

Economic Forum, June 21, 2017, https://www.weforum.org/agenda/2017/06/healthy-coral-reefs-are-good-for-tourism-and-tourism-can-be-good-for-reefs/.

8. "The State of World Fisheries and Aquaculture 2020," Food and Agriculture Organization of the United Nations, accessed April 1, 2022, https://www.fao.org/state-of-fisheries-aquaculture.

Chapter 10: The Ocean

1. Roland Geyer, Jenna R. Jambeck, and Kara Lavender Law, "Production, Use, and Fate of All Plastics Ever Made," *Science Advances*, vol. 3, no. 7, (July 2017): e1700782, https://doi.org/10.1126/sciadv.1700782.

2. "The New Plastics Economy: Rethinking the Future of Plastics," World Economic Forum, January 2016, http://www3.weforum.org/docs/WEF_The_New_Plastics_Economy.pdf.

3. Alexandra Simon-Lewis, "Humans Have Generated One Billion Elephants Worth of Plastic," *Wired*, July 19, 2017, https://www.wired.co.uk/article/global-total-plastic-waste-oceans.

4. Chris Wilcox, Erik Van Sebille, and Britta Denise Hardesty, "Threat of Plastic Pollution to Seabirds Is Global, Pervasive, and Increasing," PNAS 112, no. 38 (August 2015): 11899–11904, https://doi.org/10.1073/pnas.1502108112.

5. Emily M. Duncan et al., "Microplastic Ingestion Ubiquitous in Marine Turtles," *Global Change Biology*, vol. 25, no. 2 (February 2019): 744–752, https://doi.org/10.1111/gcb.14519.

6. Chelsea M. Rochman et al., "Anthropogenic Debris in Seafood: Plastic Debris and Fibers from Textiles in Fish and Bivalves Sold for Human Consumption," *Scientific Reports* 5, 14340 (2015), https://doi.org/10.1038/srep14340.

7. "Ocean Acidification," National Oceanic and Atmospheric Administration, last updated April 1, 2020, https://www.noaa

.gov/education/resource-collections/ocean–coasts/ocean
-acidification.

8. *The State of World Fisheries and Aquaculture 2016: Contributing to Food Security and Nutrition for All* (Rome: FAO, 2016), http:// www.fao.org/3/i5555e/i5555e.pdf.

9. "Why Should We Care About the Ocean?" National Ocean Service/NOAA, accessed August 27, 2021, https://oceanservice .noaa.gov/facts/why–care–about–ocean.html.

10. "Ocean & Coasts," National Oceanic and Atmospheric Administration, last updated October 6, 2021, https://www.noaa .gov/oceans-coasts.

11. Jenna R. Jambeck, et al., "Plastic Waste Inputs from Land into the Ocean," *Science*, vol. 347, no. 6223 (February 15, 2015), pp. 768–771, https://science.sciencemag.org/content/3^{47}/62^{23}/768. full; "10 Ways You Can Help Save the Oceans," Oceana, accessed April 14, 2022, https://oceana.org/living-blue-10-ways-you-can -help-save-oceans/#:~:text=The%20oceans%20face%20a%20 massive,And%20plastics%20never%20go%20away!.

12. "Top Ten Items," Ocean Conservancy, May 9, 2017, https:// oceanconservancy.org/news/top-ten-items/.

Chapter 11: The Poles and Global Climate

1. John Cook et al, "Consensus on Consensus: A Synthesis of Consensus Estimates on Human-Caused Global Warming," *Environmental Research Letters* 11, no. 048002 (2016), https:// iopscience.iop.org/article/10.10^{88}/1748–9326/11/^{4}/048002.

2. Ann Neumann, "Katharine Hayhoe: God's Creation Is Running a Fever," *Guernica*, December 15, 2014, https://www.guernicamag .com/gods-creation-is-running-a-fever/.

3. Richard L. Thoman, Jacqueline Richter-Menge, and Matthew L. Druckenmiller, eds., *Arctic Report Card 2020*, (NOAA, 2020),

https://arctic.noaa.gov/Portals/7/ArcticReportCard/Documents/ArcticReportCard_full_report2020.pdf.

4. Matt McGrath, "Climate Change: Last Decade Confirmed as Warmest on Record," BBC, January 15, 2020, https://www.bbc.com/news/science-environment-51111176; "Climate Dashboard: Tracking the Changing Climate with Earth Observations," Met Office, accessed August 28, 2021, https://www.metoffice.gov.uk/hadobs/monitoring/dashboard.html; "NASA, NOAA Analyses Reveal 2019 Second Warmest Year on Record," NASA, January 15, 2020, https://www.nasa.gov/press-release/nasa-noaa-analyses-reveal-2019-second-warmest-year-on-record.

5. "Arctic National Wildlife Refuge," US Fish & Wildlife Service, accessed April 6, 2022, https://www.fws.gov/refuge/arctic.

6. John Wihbey, "Pros and Cons of Fracking: 5 Key Issues," Yale Climate Connections, May 27, 2015, https://yaleclimateconnections.org/2015/05/pros-and-cons-of-fracking-5-key-issues/.

7. "Programmable Thermostats," Department of Energy, accessed August 27, 2021, https://www.energy.gov/energysaver/thermostats.

8. "Plant-Rich Diets," Project Drawdown, accessed August 27, 2021, https://drawdown.org/solutions/plant-rich-diets.

9. Stephen R. Shifley et al., "Criterion 5: Maintenance of Forest Contributions to Global Carbon Cycles," in *Forests of the Northern United States* (Newtown Square, PA: USDA Forest Service Northern Research Station, 2012), 74–78, https://www.fs.fed.us/nrs/pubs/gtr/gtr_nrs90/gtr-nrs-90-chapter-5.5.pdf?.

10. "Electricity," Project Drawdown, accessed August 28, 2021, https://drawdown.org/sectors/electricity.

INFOGRAPHICS FACTS AND FIGURES

Global Food Production and Waste

"8 Facts to Know About Food Waste and Hunger," UN WPF/World Food Program USA, August 10, 2021, https://www.wfpusa.org /articles/8-facts-to-know-about-food-waste-and-hunger/.

"Worldwide Food Waste," United Nations Environment Programme, accessed September 2021, https://www.unep.org/thinkeatsave /get-informed/worldwide-food-waste.

The Importance of Pollinators

"Pollinators Need You. You Need Pollinators," Pollinator Partnership, accessed September 2021, https://www.pollinator.org/pollinators.

ABOUT THE AUTHORS

Betsy Painter is an author and conservation biologist, who is passionate about environmental care and its faith-based dimensions. She studied religion and ecology at Yale with a focus on the natural world in the redemptive biblical narrative and its environmental hope today. On the ecology side, Betsy's research interests include wetlands  ecology, and she enjoys salt marsh implications for escapades and plankton microscopy. She attends an Anglican/Episcopal church and frequents Catholic and Orthodox churches with a passion for ecumenical dialogue about creation care and its role in fostering unity within the global church.

Josh Mosey is the author of *3-Minute Prayers for Boys*, *Dare to be a Brave Boy*, *Man of Purpose*, and *Man of Honor*. He's the coauthor of *How to Fight Racism Young Reader's Edition* (with Jemar Tisby), *The Case for Christ: 365 Devotions for Kids* (with Lee Strobel), and *Men of Valor* (with Bob Evenhouse). Josh has contributed to other books for kids, teens, and grown-ups too. For a semi-complete listing of the books he's written, visit joshmosey.wordpress.com. Josh lives in the beautiful state of Michigan with his amazing family. He enjoys turning coffee into books and learning more about God.